The Christian Counselor's Commentary

I Timothy
II Timothy
Titus

Jay E. Adams

Institute for Nouthetic Studies, a ministry of Mid-America Baptist Theological Seminary, 5640 Airline Road, Arlington, TN 38002
mabts.edu / nouthetic.org / INSBookstore.com

I & II Timothy, Titus: The Christian Counselor's Commentary
by Jay E. Adams
Copyright © 2025 by the Institute for Nouthetic Studies,
© 1994 by Jay E. Adams

ISBN: 978-1-970445-03-9 (Paper)
ISBN: 978-1-970445-04-6 (eBook)
Old ISBN: 0-889032-09-3

Editor: Donn R. Arms

Library of Congress Cataloging-in-Publication Data
Names: Adams, Jay E., 1929-2020
Title: *I & II Timothy, Titus:*
The Christian Counselor's Commentary
by Jay E. Adams
Description: Arlington, TN: Institute for Nouthetic Studies, 2025
Identifiers: ISBN 978-1-970445-03-9 (paper) | OCLC: 33193289
Classification: LCC BS2745.3 .A434 | DDC 227.87

All rights reserved. No part of this publication may be reproduced, stored in a retrieval system, or transmitted in any form or by any means – electronic, mechanical, photocopy, recording, or any other – except for brief quotations in printed reviews, without prior permission of the publisher.

Published in the United States of America

Introduction to
I Timothy

Three books of Paul are termed his *Pastoral Epistles:* I and II Timothy and Titus. They are written to ministers of the Word; not to churches (although, with the consciousness that these ministers might have to show portions of them to the congregation at some time or other). Since they are "pastoral" (shepherdly) letters, they are of particular interest to the astute counselor. "How must God's flock be shepherded?" is a question closely akin to the question "How must they be *counseled*?" In Paul's view of ministry pastoral work consists, in great measure, of counseling (See Acts 20:31). We, therefore, enter our study of the pastorals with anticipation of obtaining much valuable material for counseling that cannot be found elsewhere.

Timothy, perhaps, was the closest of the workers who accompanied Paul on his missionary tours. Though his mother and grandmother had introduced him to the Old Testament Scriptures, he had come to faith in Christ under the preaching of Paul. Paul looked on him as his spiritual son in the Lord. In II Timothy, Paul passes the torch to Timothy; he is to take over the work that Paul began. He was, therefore, a trusted disciple. But he was timid. Throughout these letters, as well as elsewhere, there are hints that Paul wanted Timothy to take a more aggressive approach to ministry. Whether Timothy did so, once Paul was removed from the scene, we do not know. But, as the result of Timothy's problem, there is much here for the reticent counselor to take to heart.

There are "inside" references that belong to those who know each other well and that need no explanation for them. For us, it might have been more helpful if they were explained. But there is nothing so esoteric that it cannot be understood—at least in part—for our purposes. This book, as well as the other pastorals, in one way or another, stresses the importance of doctrine for life. Not only do they inseparably link the two, but they emphasize the importance of healthy (sound) teaching; it alone leads to healthy (sound) living. There was error with which to contend; not in order to have one's system neatly laid out and accepted, but because the life of the sheep depended on correct teaching. This is an important message in these books.

Counselors, caught up in methodology, rather than instructed in biblical teaching, are among those who contribute to the unhealthy lives of so many Christians. In attempting to change them in ways that will please

Christian Counselor's Commentary

God, their own disregard for doctrine—as if it were something that could be neglected in helping counselees—only intensifies problems rather than solves them.

The faithful sayings that are worthy of all acceptation clearly are neatly packaged for mnemonic purposes and might even become sayings for your counselee to memorize when he faces the particular problems with which they deal.

On the whole, then, it would seem that as you peruse these three books, you should expect to glean not some, but much from them that is apropos to counseling.

CHAPTER 1

1 Paul, an apostle of Christ Jesus by order of God our Savior and of Christ Jesus our hope,
2 to Timothy, a true child in the faith: help, mercy and peace from God the Father and Christ Jesus our Lord.

As we begin to look at this pastoral epistle, let me alert you to a theme that runs throughout: What is necessary to carry on a fruitful, faithful ministry of the Word is "healthy teaching" given by trustworthy persons. Almost immediately we encounter the issue (v. 3). But, let us start with verse one.

Paul identifies himself as **an apostle** (not for Timothy's sake but) for the consumption of anyone who was looking over his shoulder as he read the letter. He wants the full authority of his apostleship to back up whatever Timothy found necessary to do in Ephesus. This apostleship was **by order of God our Savior** (an unusual expression in the N.T.; yet see Isaiah 43:3). But it also was by order of **Jesus Christ our Hope**. The two persons of the Trinity, placed in such close juxtaposition as to be the joint source of the **order** for Paul to assume the role of an apostle is an attestation to the Deity of Christ. No other name could be substituted in the verse. So, counselor, what you read in this book is clearly authoritative; there is no speculation, opinion or anything of the sort; these are the words of an apostle, appointed by the members of the Godhead to carry out the work he is doing and to authoritatively instruct those who worked with him in the matters about which he writes. You have, then, in this letter, instructions from God through his apostle about how your counseling ministry must be conducted.

God, no one less, is the One Who has brought about the salvation of His people; He is their **Savior**. And, in saving them, He has done so in **hope**. They have an expectation toward which they have been moving (Hope in the Bible is not an uncertainty, but the anticipation of something that God promised but has not yet occurred). It is that hope Timothy is to keep before him as he pursues God's work. No one can minister properly if he looks only to what transpires in this world. He must believe firmly that he works for God, Who ever stands ready both to help and reward those who are faithful. With the many discouragements that arise in the process of counseling, it is necessary to have **hope**. The counselor's task is faithfulness—learning and doing all he can God's way to further His

Christian Counselor's Commentary

> **3** As I urged you when I was going to Macedonia, remain at Ephesus so that you may give orders to certain persons to stop teaching different doctrines,

work; it is God's task to bring results. The minister of the Word is just that—a minister; the Holy Spirit is the One Who takes that Word and applies it to the lives of those with whom he works. The Word is *His* sword with which *He* fights. You must not become discouraged when you fail. God can use even your most meager efforts if He wishes. Now, of course, that gives you no excuse for sloppy work. Your task is to minister the Word faithfully and effectively. Then, in good conscience, you can leave the rest to Him.

The letter is sent to **Timothy, a true child in the faith**. By these words Paul is commending Timothy's genuineness and, at the same time, reminding him that he is a convert of his; he is Paul's spiritual child (a **child in the faith;** cf. Philemon 10). He wishes Timothy help, mercy and peace from the Father and from the Son (once again linking the two Persons of the Trinity). Every counselor knows the importance of these three elements: **grace** (here in the sense of help) since we are so foolish and ignorant; **mercy**, since we make so many mistakes and fail so often and so miserably; **peace**, since there is much to trouble the heart of the faithful counselor. Surely, these words also apply to all today who seek to faithfully minister the Word to needy people.

Now, to the epistle proper. A reminder to Timothy at the outset: Do **as I urged you** before. What was that? **To remain at Ephesus.** Why? **To give orders to certain persons** to cease and desist their activities there. What was it that they were doing? Two things are mentioned as a summary of their harmful activity: they were **teaching different doctrines** and they were **paying attention to myths and endless genealogies**. The problem that Paul anticipated has become a reality (cf. Acts 20:29, 30). False teachers had arisen and were affecting the life of the Ephesian church. The counselor who, like Paul, counsels regularly with deep concern for his counselees (Acts 20:31; "with tears"), will be concerned about teachings that would distort the viewpoint of those he counsels and lead them into dangerous paths. He will take time and make the effort, as Timothy was instructed, to do something about this. Someone (rightly) has said "Every counseling problem is at bottom a doctrinal problem." If that is so, then right doctrine, which inevitably effects living, is essential. Truth is not merely an academic matter; it is eminently practical. Good

I Timothy 1

4 and stop paying attention to myths and endless genealogies that promote farfetched ideas rather than God's program which is furthered by faith.

---

counselors, like Paul, therefore, concern themselves with correct teaching.

Timothy, with full apostolic authority (now you can see why verse one takes the official form it does), was to **order** these unnamed persons to **stop** giving such instruction. In all of this, please do not miss the note of authority that runs throughout. Apostolic counseling was not of the mamby-pamby sort that we see everywhere in today's church. Authority—the authority of Christ—was clearly exercised. It did not always succeed in accomplishing its purpose right away, but it carried with it the hope of blessing and the threat of sanction. While we must never become authoritarian, abusing true authority, we could use more of the right sort of authority in today's church. And, specifically, it is desperately needed among biblical counselors. You need to say "Thou shalt not..." and "Thou shalt..." whenever God's Word does; not something weaker. After all, you have the very same books that New Testament ministers like Timothy followed. Therefore, when speaking biblically, you are no less able to speak with authority than Timothy was.

The **myths, genealogies** and the like, mentioned in verse 4, were occasioned by many of the pseudepigraphal writings that appeared after the writing of Malachi. In them, you find a wealth of foolish material that to give serious consideration not only would waste one's time, but would lead him into endless speculation and false doctrine. What this **apostolic order** amounts to is to **stop** teaching anything that is not biblical. Could we apply this today to counseling theory? You'd better believe it! Where else can you find as many myths and endless speculations? Over 250 views of counseling in this country alone! Why no one has enough time to read them all, let alone determine what (if anything) is true or false.

What should be taught? The things of the Bible that **further God's program;** these are the things that promote saving and sanctifying **faith.** God places the very same agenda before those who minister in His Name today. Anything that fails to promote faith is wrong. Counselor, are you involved in the strange mythologies of Freud or Jung? The speculations of many others? Then, cease and desist. Learn how to counsel biblically.

Because heretical teaching contaminates **the heart,** ruins **the conscience** and leads to **hypocrisy,** Paul turns Timothy to the Scriptures. The sum of what he has to say, notice, is that (as we indicated above) doctrine

> 5 Now the aim of this authoritative instruction is love that comes from a clean heart, a good conscience, and genuine faith.

affects life. Paul summarizes the opposite effects brought about by the loving administration of the Word of God.

The authoritative instruction that his letter contains (v. 5) will promote love, which, in turn, promotes clean hearts, good consciences and genuine faith. Those are the things that every true counselor wants to see growingly exhibited by his counselees. So, he is warned, with Timothy, to stay away from those things that are not authoritatively commanded in the Bible.

The **aim** of the letter of Paul was expressed in verse 5. These false teachers, **by taking poor aim,** have sent their missile flying only to find that they **have missed** the three results of the healthy teaching listed above. They have been concerned to find out what couldn't be found out, to pursue empty activities that produce nothing worthwhile, and, as a result of aiming at the wrong target, failed to engender love. It never was the aim in view. Your aim in counseling, however, unlike theirs, must be to produce biblical love in your counselees. If love, as defined in the Scriptures ("if you love Me, keep My commandments"), is not the result of your counseling, either you or the counselee (or both of you) have been aiming poorly. Your target, **always,** must be love. The **discussions** in which these false teachers engaged didn't go anywhere (Paul calls them **empty**). Be sure that discussions in every counseling session move at least one step closer to the goal—love.

A good way to evaluate your counseling is to ask yourself "How much change have I seen in my counselees in terms of love?" Since love begins with giving, ask "Have they become more giving in their relationships?" And, in thinking about love, run the three tests of verse 5 past those cases you review. If there is little love manifest, then, perhaps, you need some biblical archery lessons! After all, Jesus said that love is the sum of the Old Testament; here, it seems that since it is to be the **aim** of N.T. **authoritative instruction**, it is also the *sum* of the New.

There are people today who, in the realm of counseling, also fit the description given of the false teachers (see v. 7). They want to be Christian counselors, but because they are filled with psychological ideas and have little knowledge of the Bible, fail **to understand the words that they speak or the things they insist on with such assurance.** Of course, Paul was speaking of Jewish legalism and the like, but the analogy to

I Timothy 1

6 Certain persons, by taking poor aim, have missed these things and have turned aside to empty discussion,
7 wanting to be teachers of the law but not understanding either the words they speak or those things that they insist upon with such assurance.

---

counselors, who speak the strangest things today in the Name of biblical counseling, is not strained. Scripture passages are stretched out of shape, made to teach what they were never intended to say and are used out of context as mere illustrations and slogans rather than as the authoritative Word of God. I have gone into detail about these errors in many other books and will not expatiate further here.

The word used in verse 7 for not "understanding" is a term that means "to not give adequate care to" something. That is precisely the problem. Like those listed in II Peter 3:16 they are careless in attaining an understanding of the Bible and, as a result, they find the most extraordinary things in the Bible—things their own imaginations first poured into its pages. No wonder, then, when they go to the well they draw out buckets full of what they want to find. Those who truly wish to understand the Bible correctly and to use it aright may do so. In II Timothy 2:7 (q.v.) God graciously promises that you can.

Now, those who have been distorting the law (O.T. Scriptures) as Paul has indicated, by their failure to use it appropriately, don't destroy the law for those who use it properly. But it must be used lawfully if it is to profit one spiritually. The problem was not that they had been ignoring the Bible, but that they did not understand it. The used it in a superficial way, adding to it in an unholy mixture all sorts of apocryphal ideas and teachings. It was the problem of eclecticism, which always leads to a failure to use the Bible carefully. Why? Because the eclectic attempts to integrate the Bible with something that is not biblical. The very same thing has been going on in Christian circles today: people have been superficially uniting biblical passages with pagan psychological dictums and assuring those who don't know better that the two are the same. The fact of the matter is that when one examines the biblical teaching carefully for what it is, there is no similarity to be found. Proper canons of interpretation alone eliminate most of the so-called likenesses of biblical teaching to extra-biblical dogmas. Counselor, your task is to know your Bible in such a way that you interpret it accurately; then you will not fall for destructive eclecticism. If you have never taken a course in Bible interpretation or hermeneutics, you ought to do so.

8 Now we know that the law is good whenever a person uses it lawfully,
9 aware of this, that the law was not laid down for the righteous but for the lawless and rebellious, for the ungodly and sinners, for the unholy and profane, for those who murder fathers and those who murder mothers, for murderers in general,
10 for the sexually immoral, homosexuals, kidnappers, liars, perjurers, and everything else that is opposed to the healthy teaching

---

A **lawful** use of the law in the context of the letter at hand was to use it not for the purpose of condemning the **righteous** who were freed from its condemnation by Christ, but to bring conviction of sin to those who are **rebellious and lawless, ungodly and unforgiven sinners, unholy and profane persons,** and all the rest mentioned in verses 9 and 10. It was this misuse of the law that was uppermost in Paul's thinking. Evidently, people could go on speculating about how the law supported their strange theories, without lives being changed. And, they distorted it in ways that judged and condemned. The list of sinful lifestyles listed in verses 9 and 10 are all the opposite of love, the true aim of the law.

The list is instructive, and useful to show how people who claim to be biblically knowledgeable, but whose lives are entirely out of accord with the aim of the Bible, are wrong. Use it forcefully for exposing hypocrisy and superficial Christianity (if, indeed, it be Christianity at all). All these things, says Paul, are **opposed to the healthy teaching**, that God **entrusted** to him (v. 10). That teaching (contained in his epistles) was to accompany the glorious good news he preached. The gospel is not freedom from responsibility; a kind of libertinism. It affects life in ways that lead toward love and away from the things mentioned in verses 9 and 10. It is a shame that such things had to be explained in such detail, but the propensity of people—even Christians—seems to be to misunderstand. And the misunderstanding seems often to be in the direction of license rather than biblical liberty.

The word **entrusted** is significant. Paul will speak of trust later on in this chapter and in II Timothy as well. He saw his ministry as something God entrusted to him and as something over which, therefore, he held a sacred stewardship. He dared not fail in his exercise of that trust. Too often, the light and even flippant manner in which the Scriptures are handled, and the consequent ruin of many counselees' lives, is found to be par for the course in much modern, so-called Christian counseling. And in speaking to its devotees about their use (misuse) of the Bible one often

11 that was entrusted to me in the glorious good news from the blessed God.
12 I thank Christ Jesus our Lord Who strengthened me, that He considered me trustworthy, appointing me for service,
13 although prior to this I was a blasphemer and persecutor and a violent person. Yet I was shown mercy because ignorantly I acted in unbelief,
14 and our Lord's grace overflowed with faith and love in Christ Jesus.

---

finds that there is little concern to understand the intent of the Holy Spirit in any given passage. The Scriptures are simply "used." Far more serious than wife abuse or even child abuse is Scripture abuse. While focusing on things like the former, they seem to totally ignore the latter. To find proper meanings and uses seems to be unimportant to them. In other words, they do not see that properly using the teachings that accompany the gospel message is a sacred trust.

Think about your use of the Bible. How many solid commentaries, Bible Dictionaries and other reference works do you own? Do you use them every week? Are you ever enriching your understanding of the Bible by digging out new truths? How serious are you about your interpretation and use of the **teachings?**

Beginning at verse 12, Paul tells Timothy about his own relationship to God and the importance of being **trustworthy** in it. His heart is overwhelmed with gratitude as he writes; he is **thankful** that in spite of his past (v. 13), by God's **overflowing grace** (v. 14), he has become a person God now considers trustworthy. He entrusted Paul with the **ministry** of the gospel to the gentiles (v. 12). Mercy was shown Paul because he needed it (he was ignorant of God's truth, despite his great learning) and unbelieving (v. 13). His zeal led him to persecute the church in violent ways (Cf. Acts 8:1). Yet, because God is able to do so, He made Paul the greatest exponent and defender of the faith he once persecuted. He became utterly faithful to that trust.

Despite the great learning of many Christian PhDs, who practice the tenets of one or more psychologists, they are ignorant of what the Scriptures have to offer in terms of help in enabling persons to change. They are equally as unbelieving when told that the Bible is sufficient and, in their own ways, persecute those who hold such views. Yet, God can turn them around. Perhaps some such will read these lines, and, by His grace, rethink their ministries.

When God turned Paul around, it was to a life of **faith and love;** traits the very opposite of those he exhibited before. In his many letters,

15 The saying is trustworthy and deserves full acceptance that "Christ Jesus came into the world to save sinners," of whom I am the worst.

16 Yet it was for this very reason that I was shown mercy so that by me, the worst of sinners, Jesus Christ might display His perfect patience as a pattern for those who are coming to believe on Him for eternal life.

17 Now to the King of eternity, incorruptible, invisible, the only God, be honor and glory forever and ever. Amen.

---

that faith and love shines forth. Moreover, it is seen preeminently in Luke's account of his ministry in the Book of Acts. If faith in the Scriptures to change counselees along with love for them and their Lord, do not characterize your ministry, take time to ask why. It may be that, like Paul, **in ignorance and unbelief** about what God's Word can do, you are bypassing the one source of help for true counseling.

Paul considered himself the **worst of the sinners** that Jesus Christ came into the world to save. Those words were not written out of some sort of false humility. Paul believed it, and in his mind, he could think of nothing worse than the life he led prior to his conversion. So, he quotes one of the several **faithful sayings** that appear in the pastorals. These were sayings or portions of hymns that were commonly known by believers. They would ring the bells for his readers. But, note, he adds the element about his own worthlessness, putting his own twist on the saying. That was using the saying for a purpose; not merely repeating it.

But why? What does Paul have in mind? He wants to show how great God's mercy is—it could reach even him. And it could turn him into a proponent of the faith he once despised and tried to stamp out (vv. 15, 16). That means that counselors (and counselees) may not despair. If Paul could be converted, retrained and used so mightily, so can you be used in God's ministry of the Word. He points out that he had become a pattern to show what Christ's **perfect patience** was like. God waited out Paul's bitterness against Christianity until the appropriate time to bring him to Himself. And He can do the same for those who are now **coming to the faith**. This patience of God is known not only in waiting for the elect to believe, but for believers to become trustworthy servants of His.

In verse 17, Paul bursts into one of his frequent doxologies. He cannot think about the grace and mercy of God without doing so. The words of the doxology honor and praise the person, work and nature of God. Paul can't get over what God has done for him. Can you? Do you still thrill with gratitude at what God has done for you—an undeserving, condemned sinner? Or have you lost the wonder of His grace? Worse still, did you never have it? Without such an attitude, you will be harsh, unfeeling,

I Timothy 1

18 This authoritative instruction I entrust to you, Timothy, my son, in agreement with the prophecies about you that led me to you, that by their encouragement you may fight the good fight,
19 retaining faith and a good conscience which some have thrust aside, thereby making shipwreck of their faith.
20 Hymenaeus and Alexander are among those to whom I refer; I have handed them over to Satan so that they may be taught by discipline not to blaspheme.

---

and cold toward those whom you counsel. But, realizing all God did for you, you will speak with joy and enthusiasm about the possibilities to which one may attain by God's grace.

Paul entrusts to Timothy the same **authoritative instruction** that was **entrusted** to him. He knows by special revelation that Timothy is to succeed him as leader of the ministry to the gentiles. Even now, therefore, in part, he is beginning to let go of the work, placing it into Timothy's hands. In II Timothy we shall see the complete transfer. You don't have special revelation so as to encourage someone to get ready to **fight the good fight** that you have been waging, but do you have someone in mind who might fill that space? Shouldn't you train him, invest time in him, help him to become all you have been and turn over some of your work to him? The training of men for the future work of ministry is vital. That is also a part of your task.

But, if Timothy is to **fight** successfully, he must **retain faith and a good conscience**. He must be wholly committed to the work, must never doubt that God has called him to it and must lead a life that he, himself, knows exemplifies what he is teaching. These teachings must be "healthy" words from one who leads a spiritually healthy life. Not like Hymenaeus and Alexander whom Paul found it necessary to put out of the church so that Satan (into whose authority he delivered them) may teach them the error of their way by the discipline of his rough treatment. By this, they will learn not to use hard words (blaspheme) against the gospel and those who teach it. Church discipline is delivering those who refuse to submit to the rightful authority of the church into the hands of Satan. Even then, at this last stage of church discipline (see Mt 18:15ff. for the various stages), the purpose is still remedial. Every counselor must become familiar with the ins and outs of church discipline because, as this verse demonstrates, there are some who by their arrogant words and actions, refuse to obey the authority of the officers of the church. Repentance readmits them into the church with all her protection and blessings. For more, see my *Handbook of Church Discipline*.

Chapter 2

1 First of all, then, I urge that requests, prayers, petitions and thanksgivings be made for all sorts of persons;

The words **First of all...** indicate that Paul is now through with the preliminary matters—though not unimportant ones—found in Chapter One. In the churches, among the members as well as among those who have the rule over them, Paul wants to develop a concern for the kind of civil government under which they live. Therefore, he urges that **prayers be made for all sorts of persons** (v. 1), including governmental officials (v. 2) *in order that* believers may **live a peaceful and calm life in all godliness and seriousness.**

The motive behind these prayers is interesting. Various people, as well as those who rule over them, may so stir up strife, hatred and trouble in a land that the church is adversely affected by it. Though we often make the point that the church is a light for a dark place, it is nevertheless true that turmoil usually has a bad effect on the church. Calm and peaceful living, such as that which is enjoyed when rulers do not exploit their subjects and officials steer clear of war, is conducive to the preaching of the gospel—and, especially, to counseling. There are better opportunities to help people when one is not, himself, engaged in survival. Doubtless, the second world war brought on many of the ills that we are still combating today. And it may have been that the Church in America (as well as elsewhere) failed in its duty to pray for those in authority so that calm and peace might ensue. Will we fail again?

Anyway, what is true on the larger scale, is also true on the lesser one. You, your congregation, and the counselee himself should be urged to pray as these two verses indicate. It is not only in the larger issues, occasioned by public decisions of the higher powers, that contribute to turmoil, but, also, on the local, more insular scale, in which your counselee moves, all sorts of persons can cause trouble. Verse one makes it very certain that we should pray for any and all, who have the power and influence to do so, that they may not. Is there enough prayer for the counselees, and those in their immediate contexts, incorporated into your counseling practices? It is rightly directed, being properly occasioned? If not, it is time to work out a scheme for introducing and maintaining it. Perhaps you might form a special group of persons who would undertake

I Timothy 2

2   for kings and all who are in high positions, so that we may lead a peaceful and calm life in all godliness and seriousness.
3   This is good and acceptable before God our Savior,
4   Who wants all sorts of persons to be saved and to come to a full knowledge of the truth.

---

to pray regularly for your counseling and counselees. If so, here is one thing you can enlist them to pray about.

But, notice, prayers should be of all types: **requests, prayers (in general), petitions and thanksgivings.** Those categories include general, specific, fervent, urgent requests—as well as thanksgiving. You may have to feed encouraging information to the group (while not revealing who it is you are counseling, or about what) so that they may see the results of their prayers and grow encouraged and thankful for God's answers. This is a delicate matter and caution should always be observed so that nothing personal ever leaks out. The sort of thing you might say to the prayer group is "Well one of the cases is developing well; it looks as if we will be finished in a week or two. There is much to praise God for." But do not say, "Well, Mrs. Smith has finally gotten back with her estranged husband. Give thanks for that."

God is pleased with such prayer (v. 3). That must never be forgotten. It is not the counselee or the church that should be uppermost—as vital as the calm and peace they need is—but, above all, prayer should be offered *because it pleases God*.

In particular, it is prayer for the salvation of individuals and officials that Paul has in mind. He **wants all sorts of persons to be saved,** Kings, and all in high positions as well as other sorts of people. That is a vital fact to remember. Often, we complain about those in high positions, but we do little about it. The average person asks, "Well, what can I do anyway?" Here is the answer. God, who brought Nebuchadnezzar to his knees, is greater than any individual and can surely intervene in the life of high officials in our country today. Instead of wasting breath on complaints, it would be better to breathe petitions for the salvation and direction of those in power, **that we may lead a peaceful and calm life.** Since God has chosen to save men and women by human instrumentality, in answer to prayer and the preaching of the Word, as a part of His providential governing of the world, it is up to His people to pray for their salvation. Here is the warrant. Have you ever asked your counselee to pray for his or her boss' salvation? Good homework given to a counselee often

5 There is one God and one Mediator between God and human beings (Himself a human being), Christ Jesus
6 Who gave Himself as a ransom payment for all sorts of persons, a fact witnessed to at the right time,

---

will include prayer for key persons (on the use of homework, see my book, *The Christian Counselor's Manual*).

You will notice the translation, **all sorts of persons** (vv. 1, 4, 6). The KJV (**all**) is manifestly wrong. If God wants *all* to be saved, they will be. God is never frustrated. But, all are not saved, as the Bible makes very clear. That is not the point; here Paul is saying, "Pray even for kings and those in high positions because God wants to save people of every sort— *even politicians!"*

Moreover, we might ask, why would Paul introduce the idea of **One Mediator** (v. 5) into the discussion? Because he has stressed the variety of persons that God is intent on saving. He wants to emphasize the fact that though there are people of **all sorts** that will be saved, they all must be saved the same way—by faith in the **One Mediator** (there is no other) **between God and human beings, Christ Jesus,** Who, Himself, is **human**.

The unity of the body of Christ is thus emphasized; a factor that needed to be stressed to many counselees who, because they didn't like something that happened at their church, have either been sabotaging its ministry or have left with bitterness and resentment in their hearts. Counselors deal with such problems all the time. One of the things they should mention is that since there is only **One God and One Mediator**, there is only one way of salvation. Therefore, counselees stand on the same ground with those they criticize. In heaven they will have to get along with each other; it is time to begin right now.

Christ **gave Himself as a ransom payment for all sorts of persons** (v. 6). The word ransom payment has in it the idea of the substitutionary atonement since one of the elements in this compound noun is *anti*, which means "instead of." The voluntary death of Christ (He **gave Himself**) is a **fact** to which God has had His witnesses testifying ever since. **At the right time** means when in the fullness of time Christ Jesus came and paid the price. Paul is a premier witness of the death and resurrection of the Savior as he goes on to tell us in verse 7. But, first, consider this: God does everything according to His timetable. *His* time is the *right* time. How strange it is that counselees often complain that what they want isn't

I Timothy 2

7 for which I was appointed a preacher and an apostle (I am speaking the truth; I am not lying), a teacher of the Gentiles in faith and truth.

---

happening soon enough. If they have prayed, asking God to do something, they should be content for Him to do it in His time. After all, that is the **best** time because it (and no other) is the **right** time.

Consider another fact: God has a timetable. He operates according to schedule which, in part, He announced beforehand by His prophets. The very years of Christ's birth and death were prophesied, as well as many other events in his life and ministry. Someone has said that, lumped together, you could give a full sketch of Jesus' life and ministry from the prophecies in the Old Testament. Well, if God works according to a prearranged schedule, who are you to think that you or your counselees have no need of one? Many counselees are confused about their lives; they are adrift. One of the reasons is that they fail to set goals and objectives, neglect to schedule those that they do decide upon, and when they do schedule, simply disregard them and do something else. Most counselees who are otherwise disorganized could also profit greatly from the use of a schedule. But, you must insist not only that they produce it, but also that they keep it!

Paul was **appointed** (set, or ordained) **a preacher and an apostle**. No one should take the preaching office upon himself. Apart from the proper concurrence of the Church, issuing in ordination (or **appointment** to the work) he is acting in a lawless manner. That Paul adds **I am speaking the truth; I am not lying,** was not to reassure Timothy. He knew that Paul's assertion was true. Again, this is one of those comments made for those who would be reading Timothy's letter over his shoulder.

Sometimes it is important to say things to your counselees that are not really for their benefit, but are of importance to those to whom they will report them when they leave the counseling room. Keep in mind any key persons who may need to receive a message obliquely. To be sure that it is repeated accurately, you might include it with some written homework assignment if you can find a way in which to insert it without being too obvious. At other times, you may have to repeat it with emphasis several times during the session.

Paul's ministry, as he often said, was to the Gentiles. He was aware of precisely what he had been called to do and never lost sight of it or wandered off the course Christ set for him. And, what he did was to proclaim the **truth** that issued in **faith** in those whom the Holy Spirit quick-

8 Therefore, in every place, I want men to pray without anger or arguing, lifting up holy hands.

9 So too, women should beautify themselves in attractive clothing with modesty and moderation, not with braided hair or gold or pearls or costly clothing,

10 but with good deeds that match women who claim to be religious.

---

ened (i.e., gave life to believe). Sometimes counselors become sidetracked. They swerve from the course they were enlisted to follow. They may become more interested in side issues, concerns of the counselee that have little or nothing to do with his problem. Thus they fail to maintain their trust. The sidetracking is not always at their initiative. Counselees, themselves, often try to get counselors off the track whenever they approach sensitive issues. Stick to the purpose at all costs.

That he has not changed the subject in the intervening verses becomes clear when we read in verse 8 the word **Therefore** and go on to hear him speak once again about **prayer**. **Lifting hands** in prayer to show that they were **holy** was a custom in that day that might well be followed today. The **men** (they are singled out because they lead the congregation) who pray must avoid **anger and arguing**. When they come to God in prayer, they should come as children who have reconciled their differences with one another. They should not expect to receive anything from the Lord if they disobey this order.

How like counseling this letter is! Paul knows people. He knows that they will attempt to get God's ear when they have just been shouting obscenities in a brother's ear. What is needed in counseling is less prayer of that sort and more that is born out of thanksgiving after reconciliation has been effected.

Well, so much for the men. What of the women? Verses 9-15 tell us what they need to know. Just as men are to pray in the service, so women are to come to church **beautified,** but not overdone (v. 9). While the clothing should be attractive, it should not be immodest or excessive. It should not, for instance, be of the sort seen in those days—the **braiding of the hair** with finely-spun **gold** mesh, studded with costly **pearls.** And the dress itself should not be **costly**. Rather than any sort of stringent ideas about clothing, these are reasonable and show good taste. That is what God wants in the lives of holy women as they come to church. And (v. 10), above all, their lives should be filled with **good deeds that match** such simple beauty.

I Timothy 2

11 Let a woman learn in silence with complete submissiveness.
12 I don't permit a woman to teach or to exercise authority over a man but to remain silent.
13 Adam was formed first, then Eve;
14 and Adam was not deceived, but the woman being entirely deceived fell into transgression.

We turn now to a very important consideration in this day of women's liberation and feminism (vv. 11-15). Written in a period in which women were asserting themselves in ways that were disruptive to the good order of the church (cf. I Corinthians 14:34), Paul goes to the heart of the issue. Women are to **learn in silence with complete submissiveness**. They are to refrain from calling out questions and causing disorder in church services. And, if told about this, they must be **submissive** to the exhortation.

Why introduce this? Because some, it seems, wanted to go even beyond and assume the office of bishop (or elder). Probably, that explains what (otherwise) seems to be an unnatural jump to the beginning of Chapter Three, which treats of church office. Women must not **be allowed to teach** (officially, in the assembly) or **to exercise authority** over men. They are to be quiet; to stop clamoring for such things. These two prohibitions disqualify women from the office of elder. The elder (or deacon) has two functions: to teach and to rule. Here, they are expressly forbidden to do either.

Now, of course, these two tasks are envisioned as used officially. All women are to teach children (Timothy's own **mother and grandmother** were commended for doing so) and other women (cf. Titus 2). Also, they are to rule the children in their home who are to **obey** not only their fathers, but also their **mothers**. So, the ruling and teaching spoken of here has to do with ruling and teaching officially carried on by Church elders. Calling on those elders from time to time to assist in counseling is important. And, if women object, you might turn to these verses for support.

Paul appends two reasons. It is fruitless to object that these reasons no longer hold because they were culturally-conditioned. Paul refers to the order of **creation** and the manner in which the **fall** occurred. There never were any two less culturally-conditioned events than the creation and the fall!. At creation, there was, as of that event, no culture yet. And, as to the fall, what little culture had developed was perfect—so no one could object that poor conditions led to the thinking.

Christian Counselor's Commentary

15 But she will be saved through the childbearing, if they continue in faith and love and sanctification with good sense.

No, the order of creation exhibits how God determined to set the roles of man and woman in His world. Man, as the **first created**, was in charge of the world, the head of his home and the church (which then existed only in embryo) And, indeed, it was the **woman** who **was deceived;** Adam entered into the sin with his eyes open. It is interesting how many cults since then have been begun by women, also deceived by error. Is that because women have tried to teach the man rather than to submit to his headship, not only in the garden, but ever since?

Well, then, what is one to make of verse 15? The word **saved** in the verse cannot mean anything other than what it has meant throughout the chapter—one's eternal salvation—despite attempts to take it otherwise. The definite article, "the," which appears in the original should not be emphasized as some have done making the passage refer to "*the* childbirth." There is no contextual referent to which to attach it. But it is not necessary, in order to maintain that the childbirth in question is the birth of Christ, to make the article have any more than a generic function. Those women who exercise saving **faith**, evidenced by **love** and growth in grace, (**sanctification**) are truly **saved** as the result of the birth of the Seed of the woman (cf. Genesis 3:15), Jesus Christ.

The role of the woman is to bring the Messiah into the world; no mean or unworthy role at all! And the birth of every child since Bethlehem should remind those who in faith have been saved that God granted this very honorable task to women—not to men. Counselees, adversely affected by women's lib propaganda, should be informed of this wonderful privilege.

Chapter 3

1 The saying is trustworthy: "Whoever aspires to become an overseer desires to do a fine work."

The continuity between Chapters Two and Three is not so perplexing as it might seem. If, as I have maintained (see comments on the closing verses of Chapter Two), the burden of Paul's words is that no woman may exercise the duties of an elder (bishop), which are ruling and teaching, then it makes sense next to determine who *is* eligible for the office. And that is precisely what Paul does in verses 1-7.

First, Paul quotes a saying familiar to Timothy, and probably to those in his church, that he declares **trustworthy**. Because it was not originally Scripture, but merely a saying (or, possibly part of a hymn) popularly known among Christians, it must have his imprimatur. By his declaration of its trustworthiness, the saying automatically became Scripture. The saying is that **whoever aspires to become an overseer (bishop) desires to do a fine work.** This saying is an encouragement for those who qualify to seek that office.

Note, the eldership is not an honorary office (though it does carry honor with it), that requires little of those who fill it. It does not merely involve one's presence at ceremonial occasions. No. As the saying indicates, it is a **fine** (the word "good" does not adequately express the sentiment of the original) *work.* What that work entails is the overseeing of God's people as a shepherd oversees a flock (for details on this point, see my book, *Shepherding God's Flock*). The eldership, when functioning well, will be involved in time-consuming, strenuous work that others often fail to acknowledge. Much is done behind the scenes—as is the counseling that is an essential part of the office (II Thessalonians 3:12, for instance). When things go wrong, the elders are blamed, whether it is their fault or not. Yet, men qualified for the office should not, therefore, shy away from it. It is, from heaven's perspective, **a fine work.** And, those who serve, must always keep in mind that it is God alone that they are serving. And He, at length, will give His recognition to those who have spent the long, hard hours spent with difficult counselees, and in meetings solving perplexing problems. Who cares about human recognition if God knows?

What are those qualifications? To be ordained (that is, set aside) to

2   Therefore, an overseer must be beyond criticism, the husband of only one wife, level-headed, sensible, orderly, hospitable, teachable,

---

the office, one must have (to some extent; no one has them perfectly exhibited in his life) the qualities listed in verses 2-7. But notice, they are not maximal qualifications, but provide a minimal standard, appropriate to a growing Christian man.

Interestingly, that with which the list begins parallels that with which it ends: **he must be beyond criticism... he must have a fine reputation.** The former focuses on that which must not be present (**criticism**) while the latter focuses on what must (**a fine reputation**). Together, they strongly insist on the same thing: anything that would scandalize the office disqualifies (until such time as it possibly may be lived down). And, among his peers, the candidate for office must be exemplary.

Interestingly, that very qualification can become a source for unfair criticism. How often have you heard God's servants unjustly charged with thinking they were "holier-than-thou?" Certainly there may be times when the charge is just. In such cases, Paul's qualification rules them out. Yet, most often, the criticism is leveled at a counselor when another wants to undermine him. Usually, this is because he is getting too close to discovering some cherished sin. So, he implies that one's concern about sin in the counselee is but a superior attitude of the counselor leveled at others to make himself look good. Often, the charge is coupled with an implication that the counselor is a hypocrite who only *pretends* to be righteous. If allowed to do so, this shifts the focus from the counselee's life to that of the counselor and puts the latter on the defensive.

How does one respond to the charge? Well, there are at least two responses that you can keep in mind:

1. As the text indicates, you ought to *be* holier than many counselees. While you will not want to make such a claim to him, or to others, your life should be of such a quality that he knows that his charge is false, and that he cannot make it stick in the eyes of others. What shows the charge to be false is that both he, and others, can see that you *do live* such a life. His objection, then, that you *only think* or *pretend* you are holier (when you are not) means nothing. The evidence substantiates the fact that you *are*!

2. Where you have failed God and/or others (and you can be sure that if he is aware of such places he will pounce upon them) don't hesitate to *admit* the fact. You will lose nothing by doing so—if you go on to say

I Timothy 3

(honestly), "But I am working on the problem. And, my friend, that is all I am calling you to do." Such a response uses his diversionary charge as a stepping stone to refocus the concern on him and his life—as it should.

Many counselees, at least for a considerable time, may be disqualified for office because the problems for which they have sought counseling violate the first / last qualification. It may even be necessary for you to suggest to some who have been occupying the office to step down until such a time as matters have been resolved in such a way that no criticism may be leveled at them. Now, of course, anyone can **criticize.** Paul refers to fair, provable criticism. But doubt, due to **criticism**, unaccompanied by **a fine reputation**, would seem always to disqualify. He must not be polygamous (see my book, *Marriage, Divorce and Remarriage in the Bible* on this point). If, instead of polygamy, Paul was referring to being married only one time in his life, he would have written **married only once** rather than **the husband of only one wife** (which for that meaning is nothing short of awkward wording). The leader of the flock must set the example in all things, including marriage. Thus, to eliminate polygamy in future generations, those who were converted as polygamous husbands would not be required to abandon their wives, but, because of the adverse example it would set, they could not enter into the office of bishop.

He must be **levelheaded, sensible**. He will have to make many decisions, based on the proper application of broader biblical principles to specific cases. He must not only know how to do this, but must do so with wisdom. The qualifications listed here are not natural ones; they are qualities derived from a study and application of the Scriptures to one's own personal life. He must not be a mere academician. He must be an all-round person, whose ability to deal with problems and people is already established.

His own life must be **orderly.** Many of those with whom he must deal in regular counseling are disorderly, disorganized and undisciplined. In order to help them, he must exhibit the qualities they lack. Not only is this important as an example to them, but because in order to help them, they are precisely those qualities that he will need in dealing with them. One whose own life is disorganized will not only not know how to help others get organized, but, even if he did, would go about it in an essentially disorganized fashion. Counselor, take heed!

He must be **hospitable.** Some people are wrapped up in their affairs too tightly. An elder must be an outreaching person. Visitors, new members, visiting preachers should all find a ready welcome in his home. Read

3   not enslaved to wine, not a fighter, but lenient, uncontentious, not after money.

III John for the opposite, from which much can be learned in a backhanded way. Such a qualification removes the crass, objectionable professionalism that some attach to counseling. It makes the counselor a human being; a Christian who cares not only formally, in the counseling session, but outside it as well. That is one benefit from the fact that counseling within the church, rather than in a counseling center, enables both counselor and counselee to get to know each other in ways other than can be known from counseling hours alone. And, for good counseling, that is essential.

Able to teach (or **teachable**). There is a debate that rages over which of the two preceding words is the proper translation. If one is able to teach, of course, he must be teachable as well. But if the word means teachable, it does not require any special ability on the part of the counselor to teach. Since many of the other requirements are minimal (not enslaved to wine, not a fist-fighter, husband of only one wife) I tend to agree with those who contend that **teachable** is the correct translation (the word can mean either). Doubtless, it is desirable, if possible, to have elders who also can teach. But there may be others, who not teachers, are good counselors, wise administrators, fine biblical, decision-makers. Can we disqualify them because they have no special ability to teach? All Christians are to teach informally. Clearly, he would be required (as are all Christians—Colossians 3:16) to do informal teaching. The elder would teach formally if the qualification requires him to teach rather than to be teachable.

There are hotheaded, stubborn persons who will have their way and brook no disagreement, who certainly fail on the count of **teachableness**. An elder should not only be able to learn, exhibiting a desire for knowledge, but should be willing to be taught by others who know more about a subject than he. Teachableness is a very important quality, regardless of how you translate the word here.

Not after money. In most churches money does not, in some special way, come into the hands of elders. Yet, he will be making decisions on how to spend money all the time. If he is a spendthrift, or a miser (both are ways in which one may disqualify himself according to this factor), he will not make good decisions. He must be one who, in his own personal life, cares little about acquiring money. If he is one who concentrates his

I Timothy 3

4   He must manage his own household well, keeping his children in subjection with complete dignity
5   (if someone doesn't know how to manage his own household, how can he care for God's church?),
6   not a new convert, lest becoming inflated with pride he might fall into the judgment of the devil.

---

day on how to make another buck, he will not make a good elder. There is more to be said on the subject of money, that we shall reserve to a discussion of the verses pertaining thereto in Chapter Six of this Book, that show clearly what Paul had in mind.

He must he a good **manager** of his home, keeping children who are in the home in **subjection,** in ways that are **dignified** (not by screaming and yelling, for instance). Here, the idea of the example comes to the front once more. But, beyond that, Paul observes that a good way to discover whether a man has what it takes to be a good elder is by looking at how he manages his home. If he can't manage the few people there, how can he manage an entire congregation (v. 5)?

The word manage is important. An elder doesn't do everything himself, any more than an efficient head of a home. He uses the resources and resource-persons God has provided to help him. In the church, the principal resource-persons at the service of the elders are the deacons (whom we shall discuss very soon). Their office is designed for that very purpose. Persons who try to do everything themselves, not only keep others from blessings, but will make poor elders because they have no vision of building up the entire congregation. They are only task-oriented, not person-oriented as well. Sometimes when one could have done something himself easily, well and quickly, it is still better to hand the task to another who is willing to learn.

He must **not** be **a new convert.** He will not know enough either of the Bible or the Christian walk in which the Bible is lived out. Moreover, as Paul indicates, it is possible for him to become **proud**, and find that his own life suffers from it. He may fall into the same **judgment** that the **devi**l fell into. In pride, he may find himself rebelling against God, wanting to put himself first.

The fine reputation, mentioned earlier, is here defined more closely than we indicated in that place. It must be recognized not only among those who know Christ, but also in the world. The **devil** has **traps** set all along the Christian's pathway. Unless he is one who has become accus-

Christian Counselor's Commentary

7 He also must have a fine reputation among outsiders lest he fall into disgrace and into the devil's trap.
8 Deacons too must be serious, not double-tongued, not dependent upon much wine, not willing to accept dishonest gain,
9 holding the secret of the faith with a clean conscience.

---

tomed to walk circumspectly, in order to avoid those traps, he may bring **disgrace** to God. How we have seen this happen in our time with many of the televangelists! Sex, money, power are among the principal traps into which many have fallen. And, on the local level, it happens all the time as well. Elders must recognize that the Name of Jesus Christ is at stake in all that they do. The office is a public office, to which people are looking all the time.

Now, Paul turns to the second, and only other, office in the Church: the **deacon**. Like elders, they too must be **serious**. That is to say, they must be men who take their faith seriously. They cannot be **double-tongued**, saying one thing to one and something else to another. Since they deal with needs of the congregation it is particularly important for them to be straightforward, sensitive and closemouthed. And when they do speak, their word must be their bond. Again, they must not be heavy **drinkers**, nor must they be involved in shady business deals. After all, they will be handling money from the church; they, therefore, must be squeaky-clean when it comes to finances.

Their profession of faith must be genuine. They must know and be able to articulate the faith to others. And they must not have doubts and questions down inside, so that their words to others occasion guilt within; they must have **clean consciences.** Counselors may be privy to those doubts and questions, which, if serious, must lead to resignation or suspension, if they cannot be satisfied. They will often find themselves dealing with anything but **clean consciences**. If these cannot be cleansed through the counseling (because of the unwilling attitudes of the counselees) sometimes, the counselor must inform the church of the problem. This may lead to suspension or deposition, if the counselee himself fails to resign or take a leave of absence in order to resolve whatever difficulties there may be. It will be the part of the counselor in many cases to thread the way through these difficulties, helping both church and counselee to find God's way.

The prospective deacon **must first be tested.** That means that the congregation that elects him must make a seasoned judgment, based on

I Timothy 3

10 Moreover, they must be tested first, then if they are free from all suspicion, let them serve.
11 The women too must be serious, not slanderers, level-headed, faithful in everything.
12 Deacons must be husbands of only one wife, who manage their children and their own households well.

---

evidence of his ability and willingness to serve. The test may be that which has been observed in the natural course of events, or one contrived for the purpose. Usually, it will involve asking him to do certain things (when he doesn't recognize that he is being tested) to see how well he serves. Again, deacons, for the sake of the Name of Christ, must be **free from all suspicion** of wrongdoing.

The women (wives, or women deacons) also must be serious, free from slander (how this can tear a church apart), levelheaded (see under the discussion of elders, above) and faithful in everything. You must be able to trust them, no matter what the issue may be. It is difficult to determine whether this is a set of criteria for deacons' wives or for women deacons. It is possible that there were such in the early church (see comments on Phoebe, who is called a deaconess, in Romans 16). Now, before you go too far and declare that Adams has gone liberal, let's think about the matter a little. There have been Presbyterian, Lutheran and Episcopal deaconesses since the Reformation; this is not a modern innovation, sparked by the women's liberation movement. It is a matter of exegesis. And, secondly, it is important to understand that to "ordain" women to the office is not some way of bringing them into the eldership through the back door. Ordination, in the Greek, simply means *to appoint to a work*. Theoretically, the janitor could be ordained to his work. The diaconate has no internal authority. It is subject to the eldership, which alone rules and teaches. The deaconate is a catchall board, created (see Acts 6) to relieve the elders from tasks that properly do not belong to their office, and that would keep them from exercising it effectively. Anything that the elders send the deacons they are to do, as the elders direct. So, since "ordination" is not the imparting of some authority, but the simple appointment to a task, the crucial question is to what task is a deacon or elder appointed? Therein comes the critical distinction.

Continuing, **deacons** may not be polygamous, for reasons stated under the qualifications for elder. They too, as **managers** of the work given to them to do by the elders, must be good managers at home. If they

Christian Counselor's Commentary

13 Now those who serve well as deacons acquire a respected position for themselves and much boldness in the faith that is in Christ Jesus.

14 I write these things to you, hoping to come to you soon,

15 but if I am delayed, you will know by them how you must behave in God's house, which is the church of the living God, as a pillar and support of the trust.

16 Admittedly great, indeed, is the secret of godliness that

---

do well, they are to be respected for their work and they will become bold in their personal witness for Christ (v. 13). This word is an encouragement for some to seek the office.

What is in this for counselors? Much about the lives of those who are the example for others in Christ's church. Looking at the qualifications for elders and deacons, the average counselee can find much to emulate. There are items here that speak volumes about how he too should live. And every qualification here is essential to good counseling. But one matter in particular should be mentioned. The word deacon, in literature of the day meant "lackey", "waiter." It is not a position of honor. The tasks that are onerous and non-flamboyant are assigned to these servants. The etymology of the word is uncertain, but it may come from two words that mean "through the dust." That indicates either that they hastened to serve, kicking up the dust behind them, or that they were the ones assigned to do the "dirty work." Both derivations fit the description of the deaconate perfectly.

Now, Paul goes on to other matters. In verse 14, he expresses his desire to **come to them soon.** But, he says, **if I am delayed,** you will know by what I am writing how a church ought to be conducted. How important, then, are the matters found in this Book. God's **house (or household)** is the church. He no longer has a visible presence (the glory cloud) in a physical, worldly temple (Hebrews 9:1). The church (the people of God, in whom He now dwells invisibly) is the repository for His **truth.** Like a **pillar or prop**, it upholds and supports the Word of God. Whenever the church in any place ceases to do so, it is no longer God's household; the glory has departed (Ichabod).

The **mystery**, revealed truth that previously was hidden, **admittedly is great.** Think about the truths that must be upheld that are listed in this confession of faith: the incarnation, the resurrection, the ascension, the fulfillment of the great commission, the universality of the Church and the session of Christ at the Father's right hand. All this is about the Savior. Any counseling affirmation, viewpoint or practice that conflicts with

I Timothy 3

> He appeared in flesh,
> was vindicated in spirit,
> was seen by angels,
> was preached among the nations,
> was trusted in the world,
> was taken up in glory.

these truths that are to be supported by the Church must be rejected out of hand.

CHAPTER 4

1 Now here are the words that the Spirit speaks plainly: that in times later on some will turn away from the faith by paying attention to deceiving spirits and teachings of demons,
2 through the hypocrisy of liars whose consciences have become as desensitized as if they were seared by a hot iron.
3 They forbid people to marry and require abstinence from certain foods that God created to be shared with thanksgiving by those who believe and fully know the truth.

According to verse one, we learn that the Holy **Spirit directly spoke** to Paul in a **verbal** manner. What did He say? That **in later times** (times not too distant) some will **turn** from the truth because they have become enamored with **teachings** that come from the evil spirit and his cohorts. He is a **deceiver,** and they will be deceived. The **hypocritical lie**s of some, who, because of their continued deception **have seared their consciences as with a hot branding iron**, will be the means he uses to accomplish his nefarious ends. Thus, without qualms, they go on spreading their lies; with consciences virtually **desensitized**.

It is good of the Spirit to speak plainly about these matters. When the apostasy of such people occurred, it would not take those who have been warned by surprise. Moreover, it gave Paul opportunity to warn Timothy and others, and help them to meet the coming onslaught. Warning ahead of time is something that the counselor must do too. While he gets no direct revelation like Paul did, he has the written revelation (including this very warning) that speaks of persecution, error, deception, lies and the like. Counselees must be told about these things that the Spirit plainly taught the apostles and that they faithfully recorded in Scripture.

What are some of the errors that they would propagate? Verse 3 clearly identifies part of their heresy as asceticism born out of Jewish legalism. They **forbid people to marry and require abstinence from certain foods.** Obviously, Paul wanted to combat this throwback to a system of merits through asceticism that many of the Jews developed during the intertestamental period. He assures Timothy that the foods they rejected were **created by God and to be eaten with thanksgiving along with others who know and believe the truth.** Nothing, he goes on to say, is to be rejected if it is received with thanks. The views of vegetarians, and those who today forbid certain meats because the ceremonial law

I Timothy 4

4 Everything created by God is good, and nothing is to be rejected if it is received with thanksgiving,
5 since it is sanctified by God's Word and prayer.
6 If you advise the brothers about these things you will be a good servant of Christ Jesus, nourished by the words of the faith and of the good teaching that you have followed closely.
7 But avoid godless and old-womanish myths, and discipline yourself for godliness;

---

did, are certainly not biblical. These verses, together with the vision that Peter was given (Acts 10:9ff), make that abundantly clear. Food is **sanctified by God's Word** (here, Acts 10, etc.) and by the **prayer** of thanksgiving with which it is eaten. All asceticism, and all reassertion of the ceremonial laws as pertinent today, is to be rejected. Counselors must set people straight about these matters from time to time. Often, influenced by Seventh Day Adventists, and others, they wonder about what they should do. Here is clear direction. Know about it and refer to it. The comment on **forbidding to marry** might well be used in relation to the Roman Catholic Church which forbids its priests to marry. From time to time, other sects (usually of a millennial sort that date Jesus' return) have been of a similar opinion. Paul divorces Christianity from any such ideas.

Notice his conclusion in verse 6 about what makes the preacher **a good servant** of Christ. It is to advise other Christians about hypocritical liars, the teachings of demons and those who deny healthy doctrine. That is quite a far cry from what the average Christian has been taught today—he thinks that talking about such things is a form of extremism or heresy-hunting. And he deplores what God commends! Make sure that your own thinking is straight about such things. It will affect how you treat counselees who have been influenced by unhealthy doctrine.

One who knows the truth and can discriminate between it and falsehood is said to be **nourished** by the **words of faith** and the true teaching that he understands well because he has **closely followed** it. According to Paul, it is highly desirable to be **closely** (i.e., thoroughly and in detail) acquainted with biblical teaching. Some are of the opinion that it takes only a passing acquaintance with Christian truth to be able to counsel. One man told me that all he needs to counsel is a dozen verses! The fact is, one must have an in-depth knowledge of doctrine to serve Christ well.

The warning in verse 7 might well apply to much of the nonsense that goes on in many counseling circles today. If much of it isn't **myth** (of the sort that **old women,** who have time on their hands, like to spread),

8 Bodily exercise has limited value, but godliness is of unlimited value, holding promise for the present life and the life to come.

9 The saying is trustworthy and deserves full acceptance:

10 "We labor and struggle for this goal because we have set our hope on a living God," Who is the Savior of all sorts of men, especially of those who believe.

---

then I don't know what it is. Freudianism and Jungianism are nothing more than mythology of the crassest type. One need not become tangled up in such things. Rather, he must **discipline himself for godliness.** Godliness comes no other way. It does not come through a formula, through a series of steps that one may be programmed to take, nor through a sudden infusion of holiness. It comes through the arduous effort that is consistently made to replace the old ways that God directs us to put off with the new ways that He directs us to put on. This requires the discipline of regularity, consistency, patience and endurance. Of course, the Holy Spirit is the One Who enables us to endure. For a longer discussion of the point, see my giveaway pamphlet, *Godliness through Discipline.*

The sort of discipline that Paul has in mind is like the discipline of the athlete. **Exercise** in the training of the **body** has a slight benefit, as Paul says (he does not despise it, but considers its benefits slight in comparison to training for godliness), but the **value** of **godliness** cannot be told. It is **limitless.** What it produces is spiritual blessing both now—in this life—as well as for eternity. That Paul makes the point that there are present benefits to godliness is of importance to your counselees and to you. Much of the focus of counseling is on present problems that must be resolved (always in the light of eternity, of course). Godliness, then, does not produce results only as pie in the sky bye and bye when you die; you can start slicing right now (v. 8)!

This important observation is followed by another **trustworthy saying** that we should fully **accept** as true: **We labor and struggle for this goal [godliness] because we have set our hope on a living God.** Whether or not one has the expectation of the heavenly reward of spending eternity with God Himself makes all the difference. It is that anticipation that enables him to endure all that the achievement of godliness entails. There is no way to become godly apart from **struggle and labor.** Those who attempt to achieve it through some formula ("Let go and let God," etc.) inevitably set counselees up for great disappointment when the failure comes—as it will. Counselees, rather, must be told that it is only

11 Instruct and teach these things with authority.
12 Don't let anybody despise your youth; rather, become a model for believers in speech, in behavior, in love, in faithfulness and in purity.
13 Until I come pay attention to the public reading of Scripture, to exhortation, to teaching.

---

through **struggle and labor** in pursuing the fruit of the Spirit that they can begin to realize what they seek.

It is God, and all that He represents, that is actually the goal of the believer who seeks to become godly. He wants to please Him in what he does and spend eternity in His presence. He is the One who is **the Savior of all sorts of people**; people from every class, nation and race, thinking, of course, of those out of each of these categories who **believe**.

It is important to talk about such matters, says Paul (v. 11); and the servant of Christ must do so **with authority** (v. 11). "But I am not an apostle who receives direct revelation from God." Oh? You have the same revelation that Paul had—*indirectly*. Timothy was to exert the authority, not simply Paul. And, if necessary, as Timothy could, you can produce the same warrant for doing so—this very verse!

There were people who might **despise** (literally, "think down") Timothy's youth, but if he became a model of godliness, it would be difficult to do so. Counselors must model what they teach. Modeling is an effective means of teaching. And, it dispels criticism, making it hard to despise the one who speaks with authority.

How can a man of God improve his ability to minister? **The remaining verses of this chapter tell you** (vv. 13-16). The public reading of the Scriptures should be considered ministry. And one should take care how he reads them. He should be sure that he puts the emphasis where it was in the original, making clear to the listener what the author's intent was. God blesses His Word, even when it is read without comment. A counselor must also read the Scriptures in counseling sessions. True, he does not read to crowds as the preacher does during the Sunday services, but, should he take less care because the audience is smaller? Certainly not; it is God's Word he is reading. Therefore, to one or to one thousand, it is important to be careful to read accurately and with expression so that the meaning is clear.

You are also to **pay attention to exhortation** This means applying Scripture to life. It is the preacher in public and the counselor in private wielding the Word of God in ways calculated to encourage the listener to

14 Don't neglect the gift that is in you, that was given to you by means of prophecy when the members of the presbytery laid their hands on you.
15 Practice these things; be fully involved in them so that your progress may be apparent to everybody.

---

make that application. It is urging the practical use of the Bible. There are those who think that you simply present the truth, and that is it. Not so. As Paul says, in the words of Calvin after him, you must put "spurs" into the truth that you teach.

He is also to concern himself with **teaching**. Most counselees need to be taught something during the course of counseling. Ignorance of the will of God, generally speaking, plays a part in most counseling problems. Because one thinks that apologizing is equivalent to seeking forgiveness, for instance, bitterness and unresolved difficulties persist. Because people are ignorant of what God has said about worry, they go on worrying all the more, sometimes even about their worry!. Some of the effective counselors I have known have a white board available on which to draw diagrams to explain some truth or other, while others scribble all over paper. In these ways, or similar ones, every good counselor that I know teaches his counselees.

In those apostolic days, special **gifts** were given (see comments on Ephesians 2:20; I Corinthians 12, 14; II Corinthians 12:12) to God's saints. Evidently, Timothy was blessed with an extraordinary gift at the time of his ordination. The presbytery (a group of elders from various congregations in a vicinity) **laid hands on** an ordinand as a sign that they had approved of his appointment to the office and that they were conferring on him the authority, rights and responsibilities of that office. The Spirit was conspicuously involved in the giving of this gift which He had **prophesied** (predicted Timothy would receive) prior to the time when it was imparted.

But, even though this gift was miraculous and directly given by the Spirit, it did not work automatically. Timothy could **neglect** the gift (by not using it, I assume). Certainly, if miraculous gifts had to be exercised, or they would become useless, your non-miraculous gifts must be put to work regularly as well. Don't do counseling only occasionally; do it regularly. Keep your hand in. See the next verse.

According to verse 15, Timothy was to **practice these things** that Paul was telling him to do. It was not enough to have ability and authority to use it; Timothy (and you) must practice in order to learn to minister well. Counseling is, among other things, an art. No artist does well apart

I Timothy 4

16 Pay attention to yourself and to your teaching. Continue in these things; by doing so you will save both yourself and those who hear you.

---

from practice. Ask a musician, if you don't believe me. How can you practice? One way is to get together with other pastors to go over various cases, perhaps role playing and critiquing them. I have published a volume that can be used for this purpose (*The Christian Counselors' Casebook*).

Next, he exhorts Timothy **Be fully involved in them** (lit., "be in them"). The original is much like our modern phrase "He's into music" (or whatever). It means that he is wholly absorbed by music; that he devotes time, energy and money to his pursuit. A counselor who is not "into counseling" will not counsel well. He should eat, drink and sleep it. His library shelves should be living proof of it. He should be consumed by ministry. The ministry of the Word is not a seven to four job. It is a lifestyle!

And, you should show **progress.** The word translated progress means cutting through what (to you) is new, virgin territory. If a man counsels no better today than a year ago, there is something wrong. Counselor, you may not rest on the laurels of the past; growth in ministry ought to be so **apparent** that it is noticed by **everybody**. If you are "into it" you are bound to grow. If you don't grow, you aren't.

But it is not enough to pay attention to the work; the counselor must pay attention to **himself** as well. He must grow as a Christian—not simply as a counselor. And, his **teaching** should improve in depth, scope and ability to communicate truth. God wants His ministers to reach for the stars; He demands excellence. He will settle for nothing else. The work is arduous, but the rewards are great—to see lives transformed by God's grace.

He is not to do these things only sporadically; he is to **continue** in them. That is to say, he is to work at them all the time, not only at certain seasons. By doing so, Paul says, he will **save** himself and those who hear him. The gospel is not a self-saving message. Paul, here, must be using the word save to mean saved from apostasy and all the other pitfalls of the ministry (cf. his use of the word "salvation" in Philippians 1:19; 2:12). And, with reference to those to whom Timothy ministers, it will save them from all the disastrous results of his failures. In ministry, what one does has repercussions not only in his own life, but also in the life of the flock to which he ministers. Therefore, it is of the utmost importance that a minister follow these directions closely.

Chapter 5

> **1** Don't sharply rebuke an older man but appeal to him as if he were your father; deal with younger men as brothers,

Now, as Paul turns away from the improvements that the minister ought to be making in his ministry, he considers the minister's relationship to various members of his flock. He begins with the older men. Instead of **rebuking** them in sharp language, the counselor of older men should recognize their seniority and respect it by the manner in which he speaks. Replace the stronger approach with a milder one, says Paul; **appeal** to him. There is every reason to think that an older believer, having walked many years with Christ, would be able to understand and follow the appeal every bit as well as the rebuke. Younger men can cause much harm from insulting those who are older, failing to respect their age. I can think of one situation in which a young preacher alienated his entire congregation (except some younger persons whom he led astray by his example) by the way in which he treated elderly men in his congregation. It was not that what he had to say was wrong; indeed, he was right. But it was the way in which he talked to them. I cringed to hear him. Talking to him did no good. He soon lost the church. Perhaps a sharp rebuke was precisely what *he* needed!

These older men are to be treated **as if** they were **fathers**. All the respect due to a father (as one who, in that role, represents the heavenly Father) must be given to older men. There is little respect for age among youth today. That is a sad commentary on our society, but one that indicates how far from the biblical ideal we have come. Surely, then, this passage is one from which not only young preachers, but youth in general, may learn something.

Timothy is to **deal with younger men as brothers**. All that the Bible says about brotherly love ought to be packed into this phrase. It means that they are to be considered on the same level as one's self. Preachers, though bearing the authority of the office, in ordinary relationships with their peers, ought not to assume some superior attitude toward them. They should treat them as those who belong to the same family—because they do! Counselor, it is easy, when a brother or father in the faith has appealed to you for help, to count him something less and to vaunt your authority over him. I am not denying that there is authority, and that there is a time

I Timothy 5

2 older women as mothers, younger women as sisters, with absolute purity.

3 Honor widows who really are widows.

4 But if any widow has children or grandchildren, let them learn to practice their religious duty to their own household first, and repay something to their parents; this is acceptable in God's sight.

---

to assert it (cf. 4:12), even as a young preacher. But normal relationships should be carried on from the basis of a brotherly stance.

The older women must be treated **as mothers** in the new Israel. Youthful counselors should relate to them as to their own mothers. And, perhaps of the greatest import, since it is the area most violated, **young women** are to be treated **as sisters—with absolute purity**. Incidentally, this passage does not forbid youthful pastors from dealing with young women, as some (overly-careful counselors) seem to advocate. Rather, it assumes that there will be dealings—perhaps even thinking of counseling situations—in which there could possibly be a violation of the pastor/parishioner trust. That is why the warning is attached (there is no warning attached to the other three admonitions). This relationship, is absolutely essential in pastoral ministry as are the other three; nevertheless it warrants special concern because of the potential problems that may arise. The wise counselor sees to it that there is an elder or deacon present whenever he otherwise might be counseling young women alone. It is not only unwise not to do so, it is foolhardy; he places his entire ministry in jeopardy.

Now we come to what is, perhaps, the most interesting section in the letter: what Paul has to say about the care of **widows**. They are to be **honored**. But, he makes it clear (by playing on the word widow which means "one who is alone") that he is talking about **widows who really are widows** (that is, those who are truly alone). According to verse 4, family members should assume the first line of support for widows — such widows are not really "alone." **Children and grandchildren** are to recognize the part these widows have played in their lives and return something to them. How often in counseling do such matters arise? How often do you turn to this passage to reveal God's requirement of children and grandchildren? If you don't, when such matters surface in counseling, you should be prepared from now on to do so. Here are concrete directions. After all, as a strong encouragement to you, Paul says that **this is acceptable in God's sight**.

> 5 Now the one who is really a widow, and has been left all alone, has set her hope on God and continues making requests and prays night and day,
> 6 but the one who lives wastefully is dead while she lives.
> 7 So, give these authoritative instructions that they may be beyond reproach.
> 8 But whoever does not provide for his own, and especially for the members of his own household, has denied the faith and is worse than an unbeliever.

But what of the widow who has no relatives, who really is alone? We are talking about a genuine Christian who prays about her condition, faithfully entrusting herself into God's hands (v. 5), not about those who, though they may be alone, live a **wasteful** life in which, while **dead** (spiritually) **live it up** (physically).

What Paul is saying, and about to say, is not a pious suggestion, it is **authoritative**. God requires it. So, then, should counselors (v. 7). These instructions are to be **given** to those involved, and to the church in general, so that all may know God's will in the matter and live in a manner that is **beyond reproach.** After all, the problem of widowhood may strike anyone, at anytime, without warning. Certainly, the Christian counselor should be prepared to guide the widow and the family through the early days of this circumstance. They may be vague about God's requirements—even if they have been instructed previously.

In verse 8, Paul makes a strong statement: Whoever will not **provide for his own** (especially when it is a member of one's own household who is involved) not only shows that he fails to understand the faith, but having **denied it** thereby, is worse than **infidels** who do provide for their own. God's deep concern about the issue ought to be apparent from these words.

But what is to be done about a widow who has no family? Beginning at verse 9, Paul details God's answer. They are to be **enrolled** by the church on a list of those who qualify. The qualifications are stated: she is to be no less than 60 years old, a non-polygamist, bearing a reputation for doing good, one who has brought up children, shown hospitality to strangers, in humility entertained the saints in her home (washed their feet), relieved those afflicted by sickness or injury (perhaps by persecution) and worked hard at (**pursued**) doing good. These are extensive restrictions and rather fulsome qualifications. It is questionable whether the average widow could be enrolled on the church's list. Moreover, in verse 11, others are excluded because of age. These widows will find it

I Timothy 5

9 Enroll a widow only if she is not less than sixty years old, was the wife of only one husband,

10 has a reputation for good works; if she has brought up children, if she has been hospitable to strangers, if she has washed the feet of saints, is she has relieved the afflicted, if she pursued every sort of good work.

11 But don't include younger widows; when they experience sensual desires they want to marry and thereby break their commitment to Christ,

12 and become guilty of setting aside their first pledge of faith.

13 Besides, they learn to be idle persons, making the rounds of people's houses, and not only idle persons, but also gossips and busybodies speaking things that they ought not.

---

difficult to remain single when they experience sexual desire and want to marry. That is a valid reason for exclusion.

But what does it mean? Why shouldn't they remarry and simple drop off the list? In doing so, they would break some special commitment to Christ that was established when they pledged faithfully not to remarry. What are verses 11 and 12 talking about? Well, it seems as if to be enrolled one had to pledge not to remarry. She was thereafter to serve Christ in some special capacity in the church, even taking a pledge to do so. If this does not speak of an order of deaconesses, as many think it does, then it does speak of some order of widows that stood in a special relationship to Christ and His church. Whatever way in which one reads the passage, he must be prepared to advise those who are cared for by the church not only of the *qualifications* but also of the *expectations* involved in that commitment by the church. It is not simply a matter of applying for assistance. Christ's "welfare program" entails demonstrable responsibility exerted in the past and expected for the future. It was neither easy to enter nor did it carelessly throw money around.

Verse 13 shows some of the consequences of enrolling those who are not entitled to support. They could learn to be idle, when they should be productive. They could become gossips, spreading information they obtained as members of the order of those enlisted, doing much harm to the church.

No, younger widows are to remarry (there is no prohibition to do so; indeed, Paul encourages a second marriage), bear children, run their homes according to the principles articulated in verse 9 and lead lives that cannot be scandalized by enemies of the church. Have you ever advised remarriage, counselor? It is one solution to the problem of younger widows that you should always keep in mind. Moreover, start younger

Christian Counselor's Commentary

14 I want younger widows, then, to marry, to have children, to run their homes, and give the opponent no opportunity for insult.

15 Already some have turned aside to follow Satan.

16 If any believing woman has widows in her family, let her give them relief, so that the church may not be burdened and may relieve those who really are widows.

17 The elders who manage well should be considered worthy of double pay, especially those who are laboring at preaching and teaching.

18 The Scripture says, **Don't muzzle the ox while he is treading out the grain,** and "The worker is worthy of his wages."

---

women thinking about the qualifications of verse 9, so that if they should ever reach the state of one who must be enrolled on the list, they will be qualified to do so. Indeed, the list of items in verse 9 is important to hold before every woman in the church. It is what God expects of them. If women are looking for something to do, here is a handful of items to consider.

The enemy has been given opportunity to insult the church and the Name of Christ by some women who have not followed these guidelines (vv. 14^b, 15). As a consequence, they have turned from Christ to pursue the ways of the evil one. Let's have no more of that, says Paul.

He turns to the case of a wealthy woman who has widows in her home. She, not the church, is to care for them. The church can carry only so many on its list, otherwise it will become overly burdened (v. 16). After all, there are those who are really widows—i.e., all alone—and the money that is available should be allocated to *them*.

Since Paul moves next to elders, and how they should be treated in the church, there is some additional support to the view that those who are enrolled by a special pledge to serve Christ, as an order of widows, may be some sort of body such as an order of deaconesses. Be that as it may, Paul does say some very significant things about elders. Those who **manage well** (the fundamental task of every elder is to rule) are **worthy of double pay**. The King James obscures the point by translating "honor" for "pay." That Paul is speaking about pay is clear from the supporting Old Testament verses quoted in verse 18 that have to do with ministerial remuneration. And, when considering the wages one receives, the church ought to look especially at those who, in addition to ruling, labor at preaching and teaching. Here is warrant for decent salaries for those who minister in Christ's name, merit raises and salaries for all elders—even those that only rule. Perhaps counselors, who recognize the financial plight of some

I Timothy 5

19 Don't receive a charge against an elder unless it is supported by two or three witnesses.
20 Those who go on sinning convict in the presence of all, so that the rest may fear.
21 In the presence of God and Christ Jesus and the chosen angels I solemnly call on you to observe these things without prejudice, doing nothing out of favoritism.

---

of their ministerial counselees, need to instruct them in these matters so that they, in turn, may instruct their congregations.

Verse 19, is an instruction you must be very careful to heed. No charge is to be received against an elder unless there are **two or three witnesses**. This is true of **a charge** against anyone (II Corinthians 13:1), but is emphasized in relationship to **an elder** since, as a leader he must make decisions not agreeable to everyone, and, therefore, he is in a vulnerable position. People who do not like what he has done may seek to ruin him by accusations. The congregation, through Timothy, is to be very cautious about charges leveled at Christ's officers. There is no doubt that, sooner or later, as a counselor, you will be brought into some conflict between a pastor or ruling elder and some member(s) of the congregation. Up front, you should make it clear that there must be biblically-adequate evidence backing up the charge (not rumor or innuendo) or you will refuse absolutely to hear it.

On the other hand, elders who *continue* **in sin**, presumably having been admonished previously about it, should be **convicted** in the presence of all the elders. The word convicted means to have a case so prosecuted against one that he is proven guilty of the offense with which he was charged. The elders, as a court of Christ's church, should hear and judge the evidence and, in accordance with biblical principles, determine the future status of the elder.

This matter, along with the evidence that led to the conviction, should be brought out before all—since he is in a position of public trust—as a deterrent to the sinful tendencies of the rest of the elders that are always present as a temptation.

Now, in verse 21, Paul gives Timothy a solemn charge before Christ and His angels (who have a particular interest in Christ's church), to be absolutely impartial in his dealings with all. There is to be no special treatment or consideration to be given to one elder over another. Because of one's position in society as a celebrity or his influence in the church or his financial prowess, it is easy for a counselor to be **prejudiced** in the

Christian Counselor's Commentary

22 Don't lay hands on anybody hastily; don't share in the sins of others. Keep yourself pure.
23 (Don't drink only water from now on; rather use a little wine because of your stomach and your frequent ailments.)
24 The sins of some people are evident, directing you to your judgment of them, but the sins of others follow later.

---

favor of certain elders over others. Let it not be says Paul! Every counselee must be treated alike.

And, in ordaining elders, there should be no quick ordinations. **Lay hands** only on those who truly have the qualifications for rule in Christ's church. If you fail to heed this admonition, Paul assures us, you will participate in the wrongs that he will (most likely) perpetrate. So, go slowly; be careful. Make sure of your man before laying hands on him (the sign of setting apart for an office). The eldership is very important in the sight of God; that is why he spends so much time laying out various specifications concerning it. Counselors should do so no less than He.

Timothy is not to become dirtied by sharing in the sins of others; he is to keep himself pure—even with reference to how he will treat his ailments medically (with a **little wine**); he must be careful not to become a drunkard: see 3:3). His use of medicine must be temperate. This says something about modern medicine and the pastor. Tranquilizers and other medicines that tend to impair judgment are to be avoided just as one must avoid the use of wine when it would do the same. Elders must not anesthetize their brains!

The sins of some people are immediately apparent. Surely, you should be aware of these in choosing elders. The sins of others, being hidden, follow only later on. I understand, Paul is saying, that you can't always be sure of every person. But, you are to make as careful a **judgment** as possible. And, there is also the fact that many good things a person does is evident from the outset; and even those things that are not will come to light eventually. So, in the selection of elders, there are matters to be taken into consideration, to be as sure as possible that the right men are ordained.

Counselors, of course, will not always be directly involved in the ordination of elders. But as they are, or even if they are, indirectly, they must contribute their knowledge of what (otherwise) would have remained **hidden**, in order to forestall the ordination of the wrong persons. The Bible never calls for absolute confidentiality. One is required

25 So too good deeds are evident beforehand, and even those that aren't cannot remain hidden.

---

only to keep matters as confidential as the Bible requires. Here wise **judgment**, based on facts—as many as can be brought to light at the time—must be made (v. 24). Counselors cannot hold back information, which, if known, they know would prohibit one from becoming an elder. They must care for Christ's Name and the welfare of His church. Counselees should be made aware of the fact that they will not receive absolute confidentially from the start, perhaps even signing a document that makes this clear and says that they wish to proceed with counseling on this basis.

CHAPTER 6

1 All who are under the yoke of slavery must regard their lords worthy of full respect lest the Name of God and the teaching be blasphemed.
2 Those who have believing lords must not show any less respect because they are brothers, but on the contrary they must serve all the better because those who benefit from their good service are believers and dear friends.
Teach and urge these things.

We are now approaching the conclusion of this magnificent letter, which contains so much that may not be found elsewhere. But, don't put down the book yet. There is still much for the counselor, in particular, in Paul's concluding words.

There is an initial word to slaves. They are to have full respect for those who have the mastery over them. There is little respect in the business community today. Even Christian people speak about their employers with contempt. That is not to be allowed anywhere—even in counseling! To allow it is to allow disrespect for God and to **blaspheme** (speak harshly) against **the teachings** of Jesus Christ (v. 1). God is not on the side of those who think they can get away with such things. Nor does He side with counselors who allow or encourage disrespect. Why? Because, as Jesus told Pilate, all authority (in business as well as in the state) comes from God and, because of this, must be held in respect—even when misused. You will have many occasions on which to explain this to counselees.

Moreover, it is important to make the point that just because their bosses are **believers,** that doesn't let them off the hook (v. 2). As a matter of fact, they should show all the more respect and work all the harder since they are **benefiting** those who belong to Christ and ought to be their **dear friends.** Incidentally, what does this say about the relationship between a Christian boss and his employee? They are to develop a warm relationship as dear friends while, at the same time, acknowledging legitimate authority and exercising it. This is a knife edge relationship. Doubtless, many will have difficulty walking the edge, but Christ expects much of His disciples. You may not settle for anything else.

Paul insists that all these things that he is setting forth in his letter be **taught and urged** on the congregation (2^b). It is not enough to communicate truth. Teachers and counselors are to **urge** those with whom they deal

I Timothy 6

3 Whoever teaches differently and doesn't agree with the wholesome words of our Lord Jesus Christ, and the teaching that is in keeping with godliness,
4 is conceited, understands nothing. He has an unhealthy desire for discussions and controversies over words, from which come envy, strife, blasphemies, suspicions, evils,
5 incessant wranglings by persons with corrupted minds who are deprived of the truth, thinking about godliness in terms of gain.

---

to observe the teachings. By the word urge, he means to persuade, to motivate, to do all that is legitimately possible to see to it that members of the congregation do not allow truth to go in one ear and out the other. Counselors, because of their intimate relationship to counselees, especially must take this admonition to heart. In the final analysis, after all else has been done to motivate counselees to do what God requires of them, there is church discipline. That is always a desperation measure, to be used after every other possibility has been exhausted, but it is there. Without church discipline to back you up, your counsel will always lack power and effectiveness.

If some in the congregation (or from the outside) try to inculcate **different** teachings, contrary to those in this letter, recognize that such teachings are **unwholesome** (and, therefore, injurious to the flock), those who teach them are **conceited** (thinking they could contradict God's teaching) and really **know nothing**. They must be ignored. All they are interested in is causing trouble. They want to dicker over **words**, cause **controversy** and bring about envy and all the baneful effects of such actions that are listed in the remainder of verse 4. They incessantly wrangle because their minds are corrupt, thinking of godliness as a means of obtaining money. We have seen enough of this in our lifetime with the televangelists who have abused their public trust. But the spirit is not absent from some less-publicized, smaller situations. You must be aware of the possibility of such persons coming to counsel about how they can upset a church in which some have stood firmly against them. They will not put it that way, of course. But they come to enlist you on their side. When you encounter those who want to fight about everything, who never let a word go by unchallenged, who always have another matter to discuss, you may well wonder whether you have such persons before you. And, when, in addition, there is money involved, you can be pretty sure of it. Be aware.

Having spoken of **gain**, his mind turns to money. Some of the most important words ever spoken about money, its use and misuse are found in

6 Of course, there is great gain in godliness linked with contentment;
7 after all, we brought nothing into the world, and we can't carry anything out of it.
8 When we have food and clothing we shall be satisfied with these;
9 but those who determine to be rich fall into temptation and a trap and into many foolish and injurious desires that plunge people into ruin and destruction.

---

this chapter. There is, of course, great **gain in godliness** (Paul is not thinking of monetary gain, but spiritual gain), he says (v. 6). This is especially true when one's godliness allows him to be **content** with whatever he has. This is true, especially, when one can be content with the basics—**food and clothing**. After all, no one brings or takes anything into or out of this world! The kind of profit that one ought to realize from his godliness ought to be of that sort. Tell this to the money-seeking counselees you encounter! And, tell them what follows as well.

In verse 9, Paul speaks of one's goal in life. Those who set the obtaining of riches as their life goal are going to experience great trouble, he assures us. They will (note: not may) fall into **temptation** and get caught in a **trap**. Many **foolish and injurious desires** will overtake them (they will never get enough) and ultimately will **plunge into ruin and destruction.**

Is money wrong? Wasn't Abraham rich? Was he ever condemned for his wealth? Note carefully all that is said and exactly how it is worded. It is those who *determine* **to be rich** who will encounter such woes. Those whom God incidentally enriches are not in view. They will be considered later on in the chapter. But what of the next verse—isn't money the root of all evil? No. Let's look at it.

If ever a verse were wrongly quoted, and wrongly translated, this is it. First, it does not say that money is the root of all evil, but that the *love of money* is what causes the problem. That is the same thing as *determining* to be rich. But there is more. The original does not say the love of money is the root of all evil; it reads, **the love of money is *a* root of all sorts of evil.** No doubt, every sort of evil has been committed out of the love of money. But there are other roots to evil as well. And, those who are **eager for money**, will find that, unless they repent and change their goal in life, **they will wander from the faith and pierce themselves through with many sorrows.** Those end results are inevitable.

When you find that the sorrows your counselees bring to you are occasioned by piercing themselves through the heart by their eagerness to

10 The love of money is a root of all sorts of evils. Some, eager for money, have wandered away from the faith and have pierced themselves through with many sorrows.
11 But you, man of God, flee these things; pursue righteousness, godliness, faithfulness, love, endurance, meekness.
12 Fight the gallant fight of faith. Lay hold on eternal life to which you were called when you made your fine confession in the presence of many witnesses.
13 I instruct you with authority in the presence of God, Who gives life to all things, and Christ Jesus, Who made the good confession when testifying before Pontius Pilate,

---

obtain money, there are few things more important for you to do than to spend some time with them discussing the implications of the truths in this passage. You have important material here for them to consider.

A pastor, especially, must **flee** from such desires. Instead, giving the put on that must replace the put off, he must **pursue** the fruit of the Spirit as the riches with which he wishes to fill his life (cf. Gal. 5). Incidentally, the fruit of the Spirit must be **pursued**. One cannot expect it to grow unless he cultivates and tends the ground in which it grows.

The ministry is a **fight**. One must agonize as in war or as in an athletic contest. It involves training and labor. But the fight is worth the effort—it is a **good** fight (one in which it is worthwhile to engage). **Eternal life** is ours now to the extent that we live a godly life. Pastors, as examples to the flock, must **lay hold on** as much of the life to come here and now as they possibly can. Timothy **confessed** faith in Christ **before many witnesses**. By doing so, he was called to lay hold on this lifestyle. Every counselee must be assured that his profession of faith implies the same. His salvation is not merely a means of escaping hell (as important as that aspect of it is) but also a matter of escaping the sins of this world as well, here and now.

To lay hold on eternal life is a **commandment** that, before God, Timothy (and your counselee) must be instructed with all authority to keep. He, the Source of such life and is the One from Whom this instruction emanates—from no one less (v. 13). This commandment must be kept **unspotted and free from suspicion**. The purpose of your life clearly must be to lay hold on eternal life—not on money. No one should be able to throw the slightest suspicion on that fact. As Christ **made a good confession before Pilate**, so too, you must do so. How easy it is for counselors to make money their object. Rather than counsel free through the

Christian Counselor's Commentary

14 to keep the commandment unspotted and free from suspicion until the appearance of our Lord Jesus Christ,
15 which in His own time will be publicly displayed by the blessed and only Sovereign, the King of kings and Lord of lords,
16 the only One Who has deathlessness, Who dwells in unapproachable light, Whom no person has ever seen or can see, to Whom be honor and eternal might! Amen.
17 Authoritatively instruct the rich of this present age not to be haughty, nor to set their hope on the uncertainty of riches, but rather on God, Who richly provides everything for our enjoyment.

---

church I pastor (at a nominal salary) I could make many times that much by counseling on my own. I realize that fact but, because I believe that counseling should be done in conjunction with pastoral ministry, I have chosen the non-lucrative route. I have seen how much others have been able to make by hanging out a shingle (some even drive Mercedes). One's motives, as exhibited in his actions, must be clear and free from the stains and spots of money seeking. Few things spot a man's ministry more than well-founded suspicion of this.

And, don't let down your determination not to pursue money, but to pursue godliness. Follow that determination until the day when Christ appears. Then, He will be publicly displayed by the Father for all that He is. God, the only Sovereign, the King of kings and the Lord of lords, in that day, will right all wrongs. He is the only One who is deathless (v. 16). He now dwells in unapproachable light (it is too brilliant to endure). No one ever has or ever can see Him (but see John 1:18). He is the One to Whom all glory and honor belongs!

But, there are people who are rich even though they did not set their hearts on getting rich. They are perfectly right in the matter. What does God have to say to them? They are to be instructed not to allow their riches to make them haughty (they must associate with all the brothers in Christ). And, they must not depend on their wealth (which is uncertain—it could be swept aside in a moment), but on God. That is the first thing they must be told. You will do well to remind the rich you counsel of these facts as well as those that follow.

Moreover, they have not been given riches only for themselves **to enjoy** (though that, in itself is not wrong; cf. v. 17^b). They must **do good** with their money. That should be one of their greatest joys. They must be **rich in good deeds**! They should **be ready to give and genero**us when they do. What a job description for you to read to your rich counselees.

18 They must do good, be rich in good deeds, be ready to give, generous,
19 laying up the treasure of a good foundation for the future so that they may lay hold on the life that is really life.
   20 Timothy, guard that which was entrusted to you, turning away from the irreligious chatter and contradictions of what is falsely labeled "knowledge,"
21 which some have professed but by taking poor aim have missed the target of the faith.
   May help be with you.

Then, they will lay up a treasure that cannot be taken from them so that **the life which is really life** in the **future** in heaven will be a marvelous one for them. What a powerful discussion of money and true wealth this chapter unfolds! It is powerful because it is so practical and it is so well-balanced. Learn what it teaches and let it guide you in every discussion of money with your counselees.

The conclusion: verses 20 and 21. Timothy, it is so easy to lose hold of the true message; **guard** it. You will be able to do so if you **turn from the chatter** of people who are presenting what they falsely label "**knowledge.**" Perhaps Paul is dealing with early gnosticism here. At least, he is concerned with those who think they have *something more or something different* to add to what he has said. What a timely warning this is to Christian counselors who are bombarded with false "knowledge" from all sides. Because they have **taken poor aim**, they have missed eternal life altogether; they are outside of the faith (Cf. 1:5). Recognize them for what they are. A somber note on which to end, that only makes the warning more pointed. Perhaps, occasionally, counseling sessions ought to come to a somber note as the final word before prayer. There are times when nothing less will emphasize what one wants to say. As Timothy was to put down this letter with that warning in mind, so too a counselee might leave with a warning he needs to heed. Take a leaf from Paul's notebook.

Introduction to II Timothy

This is Paul's last epistle. Indeed, it is his last will and testament. In it he bequeaths the ministry that was given him by God to his faithful companion Timothy, who throughout the years was ever ready to assist in any ways that Paul desired. It is a letter filled with pathos (**bring the cloak that I left at Troas; winter is near...Luke alone is with me**); yet through all rings the note of victory (**I have fought the good fight; I have finished the course**). But the letter is not simply reminiscences of the past. Paul was about to die for his Master. But he was concerned about the churches and the work that he would leave behind. What was necessary to preserve both is the concern of this letter.

There is warning about the days to come which, as a prophet, Paul knew would be difficult. Yet, as he describes those days, he might as well be describing our times. That is how up to date the letter is, and, therefore, how important to us.

The problem of fear as an obstruction to Christian living and ministry dominates large portions of the letter. Indeed, one of Paul's major thrusts is to counter such fear in Timothy. Counseling often is retarded by fear. Pastors often fear losing members if they speak frankly to them. Counselees fear doing new and hard things that God requires. Fear of other people often pervades the counseling room. Of great importance, then, are Paul's words on this subject.

There is direction about passing the torch not only to Timothy but to those who would follow him. And there is much about preserving the truth of the gospel. All in all, II Timothy offers much for the counselor who wishes to be careful about the exposition and the application of God's Word. And, in addition, it directs him through the maze of pitfalls that surround him.

CHAPTER 1

1 Paul, an apostle of Christ Jesus by God's will in agreement with the promise of life that is in Christ Jesus,
2 to Timothy, my dear child:
help, mercy and peace from God the Father and from Christ Jesus our Lord.

As he opens the letter, Paul wants to give Timothy all the authority he needs to carry out God's ministry, so he styles himself **an apostle**. Obviously, the title was not for Timothy's benefit, but for the benefit of any who wanted to know by what authority Timothy was acting: it was by apostolic authority. And he could show this letter to anyone who questioned it! The letter, together with the other two pastorals, was soon placed on file with all of the churches as New Testament Scripture. Paul knew that this would happen and its authority would be essential, so he alludes to it at the outset. It is still authoritative today.

It is wise always to let your counselees know by what authority you counsel. There is no legitimate authority other than that of the Word of God, when you come down to it. All other authority behind counseling is arrogated to themselves by counselors who have set up their own authorities. Like other biblical counselors, you alone counsel by the authority of God. Never forget that fact.

Christ is the One whose apostle Paul is, **by the will of God.** And, this is in agreement with His **promise of eternal life**. How so? Well, because it was in order to proclaim the promise that Paul was appointed as Christ's apostle. He is writing to the one he calls **his dear child** (v. 2). Their relationship was the closest. Timothy was like a son to Paul. He wishes three blessings upon him: **help** (he'd need it), **mercy** (there would be many hard times ahead and he would make mistakes) and **peace** (a contentment that transcends happenings). All these must come **from God the Father and Christ Jesus our Lord.** There could be no other source. Incidentally, the combination of the Father and the Son as joint Givers of the heavenly graces is proof positive of the deity of Christ. Try putting any other name in the place of Jesus Christ in that statement and it would be blasphemous.

Coming to verse 3, Paul begins his usual thanksgiving. But its content is unusual: not only does he mention his prayer life as the **service of worship,** but he maintains that he is in continuity with his **forefathers** in doing so. And, he prays with a clean conscience in his regular requests for

Christian Counselor's Commentary

> 3 I thank God to Whom I give the service of worship as my forefathers did with a clean conscience, when I remember you regularly in my requests night and day.
> 4 When I remember your tears, I long to see you so that I may be filled with joy.
> 5 I recall your sincere faith that dwelt first in your grandmother Lois and in your mother Eunice and I am convinced dwells in you too.

them offered night and day. That a counselor should pray like this and see his counselees in this light is highly desirable. After all, here are people in trouble who need the prayers of the one who is helping them. And, the wonderful fact is that such prayer for one's counselees is a part of one's worship of God. Other counselors, who know nothing of Christianity, cannot benefit from the blessings that this brings not only to counselees, but also to counselors. Are your regular prayers offered as worship to God as you mention the needs of your counselees?

Paul remembers Timothy's **tears**. Presumably shed at their parting when Paul was arrested and taken to prison in Rome where he was now awaiting his death. This parting also saddened Paul. So he hoped to see Timothy at least once more before he was executed so that he may be **filled with joy**. It is not wrong for the counselor to express what, in the actions of his counselee, brings him joy. It is not wrong in Christian circles to allow one's emotions to be known. It is not wrong among God's children to appeal to them on the basis of the effect their actions may have on one's self—so long as this is accurate and is not selfish.

In speaking of how he remembers Timothy, he mentions **the faith that dwelt** first in his **grandmother,** then his **mother** and, now, in Timothy as well. Here is an instance of the fact that family faith through the generations does not have to weaken, as so often it seems to. Indeed, God uses families to pass on the faith through the generations (Deuteronomy 6:1-3). That should bring hope to parents and those whose children have not yet come to faith in Christ.

But Timothy was timid. He also tended to hang behind, it seems. That is why Paul had to stir him up from time to time and to urge others to do the same. In verse 6, he says, since I believe that your faith is genuine, I want to **remind you to rekindle into a flame God's gift**. There is no doubt that Timothy needed this encouragement. Many counselees also need such reminders by way of encouragement. Part of the counselor's task is to help them rekindle the flame that, by the time they come for counseling, is virtually extinguished.

6 For this reason I remind you to rekindle into a flame God's gift that is in you through the laying on of my hands;
7 I say this because God didn't give a spirit of cowardice, but of power and of love and of self-restraint.

This was a special **gift** that, when Paul participated in his ordination by **the laying on of hands**, God gave through him to Timothy. Doubtless, since the ordination (a setting aside to a task; and appointment) had to do with the gospel ministry, the gift was one that enhanced it. But God's gifts do not work automatically; they must be kindled, and when allowed to burn low, **rekindled** again. Presumably, then, Timothy needed to develop and use his gift for ministry. You and your counselee may have numerous gifts, but if they are dormant, something must be done to stir them up again. Does the fire burn brightly in you? Do you have a task to help a counselee to rekindle his gifts *right now*?

Why did Paul bring up the matter? Well, he is thinking of Timothy, the successor to his own ministry, the man gifted to carry it on, and the failure of Timothy up to this point to exhibit the qualities necessary to do so. Why had Timothy failed? Because of timidity and fear (cf. v. 7). He says that he mentions the matter because God did not give him **a spirit of cowardice, but of power and of love and of self-restraint.** Presumably, these were the things about which Timothy needed to be reminded. His timidity, if not checked, would soon deteriorate into **cowardice**, especially with Paul off the scene. His timidity tended to make him weak rather than **powerful**. And his love was not being manifested as it should in the ministry. A lack of **self-restraint** possibly lay at the bottom of it all. He was afraid that if he did what he should, things would get out of hand. He knew his own tendencies, when inflamed, to go too far. But, the Spirit produces the fruit of **self-control (constraint)**. He need not fear, says Paul.

Well, how often are similar situations encountered in counseling? You know that cowardice often plays a role in those who fear to take those biblical steps that God requires. There is weakness and lack of love. And, frequently, you run into all sorts of problems connected with lack of self-restraint. Here, then, is a very pointed passage that speaks to each of these matters. Refer to it often. If he is God's child, your counselee has the Spirit Who can overcome each of these problems. How? By rekindling the flame of power, love and self-restraint that he already possesses by virtue of the Holy Spirit dwelling within.

Christian Counselor's Commentary

> 8 So then, don't be ashamed of the testimony of our Lord or of me His prisoner, but rather share with me my suffering for the good news by the power of God,
> 9 Who saved us and has called us with a holy calling not because of our deeds but because of His own purpose and the grace that He gave us in Christ Jesus before time began.

Those with a cowardly spirit often fail to stand up for the things of Christ in the clinch. Paul exhorts Timothy to do so: **don't be ashamed of the testimony of our Lord or of me His prisoner.** It is easy, with cowering Peter, to deny the Lord in such situations. Timothy would find himself in many difficult circumstances if, as Paul, he conducted his ministry productively. He would need fearlessness to do so. And, he must stand up for those things that he believed, as well as for his companions in the faith, even when the going gets tough.

Counselees today rarely encounter the severe persecution that Paul had known and Timothy would experience. But in various ways they do have to stand up for their faith. And they need courage to withstand ostracism and criticism when it comes their way. Again, the promise of the spirit of power, etc. (v. 7), should be effective in calling them to do so.

Now Paul makes it all clear: he bids Timothy to share with him the sufferings for the good news that he was experiencing by God's power. Paul is not ashamed (v. 12). Timothy must not be either if he is to share in the ministry of the gospel which always, in some manner or other, involves suffering. Paul did not sugar coat the ministry. He knew that it was a dangerous calling when properly conducted. But the interesting thing is that he called him to it anyway. From listening to many of the calls into the ministry today, and the conversations of those who have answered them, you would think they were entering some plush occupation. The best young men are challenged by a realistic call to experience difficulty for Christ. Never forget that in dealing with them. Such a call scares off those who do not belong in the first place. And that is very necessary. But, Paul also assures them that, with the danger, comes **the power of God** to enable the young minister to endure.

And, to remind Timothy (and your counselee) of all God did for him, he recalls the marvelous **grace** of God by which he was **saved** (v. 9). It was the One Who saved Who also **called**. That calling was **holy**. That is to say, it was one that had to do with God separating them out (the word holy means separated) for His own purposes. The calling came not because of

II Timothy 1

10 But now it has been manifested through the appearance of our Savior Christ Jesus Who (on the one hand) has broken the power of death and (on the other) brought to light life and incorruption through the good news,
11 for which I was appointed a preacher and an apostle and a teacher.
12 That is the reason why I also suffer these things; but I am not ashamed because I know Whom I have believed and am convinced that He is able to guard what He has entrusted to me until that Day.

---

works-righteousness, but simply out of God's **purpose** (His good pleasure), and the grace He gave resided **in Christ Jesus before time began**. This is a cosmic thing; something that was in God's mind from all eternity. Recognize its importance. No one working in God's vineyard should disdain the meaning and purpose of such work.

And **now**—what a privilege to be in on it from the ground floor—that purpose and plan of God from all eternity has come to fruition by the coming and work of Christ. **He broke the power of death** (by His resurrection); so what is there to fear? He **brought to light life and incorruption through the good news** (so there is much to look forward to). And I, says Paul, have been **appointed a preacher and an apostle and a teacher in order to promote that good news.** So, Timothy (counselee, counselor) recognize what it is that you are participating in. Every Christian counselor should look at his work as an exciting ministry and a privilege. He, of all people, is able to impart the truth of God's Word that, used by the Spirit, transforms life. He is able to counsel in the light of the eternal verities mentioned so triumphantly in verse 10. The excitement by which Paul woos Timothy to the life he lived, combined with the stark realism of the dangers is the right combination for helping many counselees face decisions and enter into tasks that, otherwise, they might readily avoid.

Paul returns to realism in verse 12. I do suffer because I teach and preach the gospel as an apostle of Christ. But **I am not ashamed** of the fact. Here, in prison, facing death, I can hold my head high. I serve the King of kings and the Lord of lords. Of what, then, should I be ashamed? It is He in whom **I have believed.** And, **I am convinced that He is able to guard what He has entrusted to me until that day** when He comes again.

Note the translation does not agree with the KJV or the hymn based on it. The Greek says "my deposit." If someone hands money over to a teller at the bank, he may call it "my deposit." If, on the other hand, the teller who receives it says this is "my deposit" with which I have been

Christian Counselor's Commentary

> **13** Have the pattern of healthy words that you heard from me in the faith and love that are in Christ Jesus;
> 14 guard the good deposit entrusted to you through the Holy Spirit Who dwells within us.

---

entrusted, he too can rightfully use those words. The rest of this chapter and the next make it clear that Paul is speaking as the teller, who has received a deposit of truth that, by God's ability, he must guard.

Paul now exhorts Timothy to **hold on to the pattern of healthy words that you heard from me in the faith and love that are in Christ Jesus** (v. 13). As Paul was entrusted with such words in order to preserve and teach them, so Timothy now would find it necessary to do so. If there are **healthy words**, there are also unhealthy ones. You will find that in the ministry there will always be those who want you to trim your sails. They want you to accept and teach unhealthy words that they claim are full of vitamins and nutrition. Actually, it is that which is new, that which is not a part of the **deposit** God gave, that is to be avoided. If the words are not God's words, they are unhealthy for any minister to feed to his people. Surely, there is a message here for every counselor. How many siren voices call you to depart from the Scriptures to embrace something new! Something different. Something more. Counselor, if you would do truly Christian counseling, then counsel out of the **deposit** given by God, and out of that alone.

Indeed, Paul is so emphatic about this that he is concerned not only about the deposit, but the form (**pattern**) in which it is presented. Remember how I presented the message. Imitate it. Remember the terminology I used; you use it. Counselors can get caught up in the jargon of the "profession." They make a mistake in substituting "psychological" terms for biblical ones. People need to know what God calls their difficulties, not only for the sake of accuracy and hope, but also so they can discover what the Bible says about them. When you use biblical labels, you can find biblical solutions.

And the defense of the truth must be carried on in faith and love. Not in some lesser way.

Paul has **entrusted** to Timothy what God first entrusted to him. Here is the clear indication that Timothy was to receive the torch from Paul's hands. He is to **guard** it by calling on the **Holy Spirit** Who **dwells** in Christ's church and in each individual Christian to keep him faithful.

Paul says, what I am telling you is nothing new. You already have

II Timothy 1

15 You know this, that all those who are in the province of Asia turned away from me, including Phygellus and Hermogenes.

16 May the Lord show mercy to the household of Onesiphorus because he often refreshed me, and he wasn't ashamed of my chain.

17 Indeed, when he arrived at Rome he diligently searched for me and found me,

18 (May the Lord grant him to find mercy from the Lord in the Day!) and you know very well the things he did to serve me at Ephesus.

---

heard it before (v. 15). I am counting on you, Timothy, because there are so few left. All in Asia (minor) turned away. That probably means those in Rome who were from those places. And, even two of whom you would never expect it: **Phygellus and Hermogenes**. There was, however, faithful **Onesiphorus**. May God bless his **household** because he often left them behind to show kindness to me in prison. Here was a man who was **not ashamed of my chain!** He even searched everywhere at Rome until he found me. And, his presence was like a glass of water on a steaming hot day; he often refreshed me. We don't know how, but even his presence, it would seem, was enough to bring joy and encouragement to Paul's parched soul. I wish him the mercy of God on the day of Christ. But I don't need to tell you about him; you know all he did for me at Ephesus.

Powerful material. Paul does not hesitate to name names when necessary in order to warn against some or to compliment others. Perhaps we are far too reticent in our day about such things. Think it through. There is too much fear of man as opposed to the fear of God. And let me ask you: how brightly does your flame burn?

CHAPTER 2

1 You, then, my child, find strength in the help that Jesus Christ gives.
2 And the things that you heard from me before many witnesses pass along to trustworthy persons who will be competent to teach others also.
3 Endure your share of suffering as a good soldier of Christ Jesus.

Concluding the foregoing remarks (Chapter One), Paul urges: **find strength in the help that Jesus Christ gives.** That, of course, is the final answer to Timothy's timidity. Jesus can turn a Timothy into a bold witness to His truth as He transformed the wavering Simon into a Rock. Jesus is still willing and able to do the same for you and for your counselees. How important for both of you to recognize that fact. Counseling that is truly Christian never settles for less because it is never carried on merely by the power of human strength. There is always a supernatural quality about it. That, perhaps, may be why some counselors shy away from it. Human ideas and power can be manipulated by man. But because of the divine element in true counseling, neither the counselee nor the counselor has ultimate control. He is forced to depend on the Holy Spirit. Some don't like that.

Now, Paul turns to the matter of Timothy's successors. He envisions the ministry continuing at least two generations beyond Timothy himself. Incidentally, this does not look like Paul expected Christ to return in his time, does it? Those who think that he prophesied He would, but failed, simply misunderstand the passages from which they purport to glean such teaching.

The deposit of truth Paul received he had taught faithfully to Timothy, even (as we have seen) putting it into some memorable pattern by which it could be preserved and passed on. Timothy was to preserve it, pass it on the faithful men (who would neither add nor subtract, but) who would in turn pass it on intact to those who would follow them. Have you considered the importance of teaching the principles and practices of Christian counseling to the next generation? Since so precious few do truly Christian counseling, and since it is important to convey these principles and practices to the next generation, why not teach several young pastors how to do it?

Paul is not through with the matter of suffering. He calls on the minister of Christ to **endure it as a good soldier of Christ Jesus.** The war with the forces of evil that Christ is carrying on in this world is in earnest.

II Timothy 2

4 A soldier avoids becoming involved in everyday business activities so that he may please the one who enlisted him.
5 Again, an athlete isn't awarded the winner's wreath unless he competes according to the rules.
6 It is the laboring farmer who deserves to have the first share of the crops.
7 Consider what I am saying; the Lord will give you understanding in all things.

It will not be fought by those who are not fully committed to it. A soldier leaves business matters at home behind him when he goes to war. Can you picture a soldier out on the battlefield with a cellular phone conducting business while fighting? There can be no divided loyalties in Christ's service. In order to please his Lord, he gives himself completely to the work. Words for every counselor, for sure.

Using a second example, Paul says the minister must be like an **athlete**. He wins only when he observes **the rules** of the game. All trickery, manipulation and the like must be removed from the work of counseling. One's methods must be entirely above board and in accord with the principles and practices of Scripture. His methods must grow out of and be consistent with the truth at every point. And he must be able to substantiate the fact when called on to do so.

A final example is that of the **farmer.** The farmer, deserves the first share of the crops (he should be paid out of the work itself) because he **labors** over them. The ministry is hard work. It takes effort and toil to work with people, often (because of their sin) with no tangible results. Counselors must not become discouraged, but continue laboring. In time, God will give them a crop.

If there is anything that is difficult for Timothy to comprehend about what Paul has been saying, he assures him that even this is not a serious problem. If he gives full consideration to the words in the letter, prayerfully attempting to comprehend, the Lord (through the Spirit, Who is the One who illumines the Word for Christians) **will give him understanding** about whatever he needs to know. That is a precious promise on which we may rest today. But, remember, that **understanding** comes only upon careful **consideration** of Scriptural truth. Too many use the Bible in a casual (I almost said flippant) manner, without thoroughly considering its intent and meaning, and expect to understand. The word **consideration** implies effort of the proper sort to reach an accurate interpretation of particular passages. The Lord does not gift people with understanding who

> **8** Remember Jesus Christ, as One Who has risen from the dead, descended from David, according to the good news that I preach,
> 9 for which I am suffering wrong even to the point of being chained like a criminal. But God's Word is not chained!

are reluctant to take the time or expend the effort to carefully consider what the Spirit is saying through the writings of human authors whose words He has inspired.

Now, moving on, in verse 8 Paul exhorts Timothy to **remember Jesus Christ** as the risen Savior. The One Who descended from David as the prophecies foretold, says Paul, is the One whom I preach. Paul's message is in continuity with the Old Testament. Paul could never forget Jesus, His remarkable death and resurrection (which is the good news; cf. I Corinthians 15:1-4) and what He had done for him. That is the kind of ministry that he wished Timothy to pursue—one in which Jesus Christ is the goal and meaning of it all. He knew if Timothy did, he would be able to endure what lay ahead and that if he did not, he would fail to do so. Jesus was truly the Messiah. Timothy must never forget that fact. Counselors who **remember**, bring to their counseling an atmosphere of hope, joy, anticipation and victory. They do not, as so many others must, wonder whether what they tell the counselee is true and whether it will work. They not only know that it is true, but that, if the counselee means business, he will receive personal fulfillment of God's promises.

Paul cannot help remarking again that he is **suffering** for the good news that he preached, even to the point of being **chained** to a guard with a manacle. But, as victory overcomes pathos, he virtually shouts **the Word of God is not chained**! He identified closely with the gospel, at times even calling it "*my* gospel," yet he recognized that though God had used him in marvelous ways, he was not indispensable. And, now, as he was about to depart the earthly scene, he declares, half in joy and half in assuring Timothy, that there is no restraint on God's Word. One thing that can never be done is to silence the voice of God heard in His Word. That is why, as counseling systems after counseling systems come and go, the truth of God remains; it is the one enduring system that continues to change lives where the others have failed. Counselor, if you are not already there, get on board with those who stand with the saints of every age, finding in the Bible all things necessary for life and godliness. It did not take 1900 years for the church to discover the answers to human life and its problems in some system not only foreign to Scripture but in con-

> 10 Therefore I endure for the sake of the chosen ones, so that they too may obtain the salvation that is in Christ Jesus, together with eternal glory.
> 11 The saying is trustworthy:
> If we died with Him, we also shall live with Him;
> 12 If we endure, we also shall reign with Him;
> If we deny Him, He also will deny us;
> 13 If we are unfaithful, He remains faithful, because He cannot deny Himself.

flict with It.

Why did Paul endure such hardships? To please his Lord, certainly. But he also had subsidiary objectives in mind that drove him. So that Timothy can catch something of the spirit of his ministry, and what kept him going in spite of every sort of affliction and obstacle, Paul tells him, **I endure for the sake of the chosen ones**; that is, those whom God has chosen for salvation who have not yet heard the life-giving message. He wants them, too, to have eternal life (v. 10). Election does not deny the use of means. Nor, when properly understood, does it weaken one's zeal for the lost. Indeed, knowing, as Paul does, that there are people who *will* believe only motivates him all the more to bring them to faith in Christ for salvation. If there were no assurance that God had ordained some to eternal life, so far as he can tell, one's efforts might turn out useless. Paul had no such view of things. He preached the gospel because he knew there were some out of every tribe and tongue and nation who would believe. And, he knew also that they would come by means of preaching (Cf. Romans 10).

Quoting a piece of poetry or portion of a hymn that was true, Paul declared it **trustworthy** as he incorporated it into his letter, thus making it a part of God's revelation (v. 11). The poetic portion is interesting. Echoing John's words in Revelation 20, he makes it clear that those who are martyred for the faith would **live** (v. 11) and **reign** (v. 12) with Christ. In the first resurrection (that of the martyrs) this promise would be fulfilled (On this, see Revelation 20 and my book, *The Time is at Hand*). But those who **deny Him** in the time of trial, He will **deny.** And, though men may be **unfaithful**, you can depend wholly upon Him—He is **faithful**. There cannot be any doubt about this because it is impossible for Him to go back on His Word and thus **deny himself** (v. 13). Here is warrant for the statements made above about the assurance that the counselor has that God will always fulfill his promises.

Timothy is to **remind** his congregation about these things. They too

14 Remind them about these things, solemnly calling on them in the presence of God not to argue about words, since that is of no use and tears down those who listen.

15 Do your best to present yourself to God tried and true, a workman who won't be ashamed, cutting the Word of truth with accuracy.

---

needed strengthening. And, he is to **solemnly call on them not to argue about words** (lit., to engage in word wars), since this is **useless** activity that only **tears down** rather than builds up **those who listen**. There is much in this 14th verse for the counselor. First, if anyone ever needed reminding about the truths of God it is the average counselee. **Reminding** may be irksome at times, but it is necessary. If it were not, Paul (and others in Scripture) would not have repeated themselves so often and would not urge others to remind their constituencies.

And, **arguing about words!** Word wars! Ever heard any of that in the counseling room? You'd better believe it. When people become disgusted with one another, frustrated and unproductive, they often descend to this very thing. Tell them what Paul tells Timothy: this activity is not only useless, but it **tears down others** when you ought to be building them up. Any counselor who allows battles over words to take up precious counseling time acts foolishly. The activity, as Paul says, is **useless.** A powerful verse for so many counseling sessions! Learn it and use it frequently.

Your task is to use the Scriptures in a mature and helpful manner. To that end, you should do all you can to **present yourself to God tried and true, a workman who won't be ashamed, handling the Word of truth with accuracy.** That means that as a workman, sawing or chipping and fitting pieces of lumber or stone, he must be sure that his cuts are straight. So too must the Biblical workman in the Word cut and fit passages to people in various circumstances with similar accuracy. Otherwise, he will someday be ashamed when the Lord speaks to him about how he handled His Word. Your ministry should be characterized by accurate and effective use of the Bible. Surely you must learn how to find the right biblical board or stone to fit the counseling situation and, how to explain and apply it to those involved, never misusing one verse. That should be your goal. To be able to do so, you must spend much more time doing biblical interpretation than the time you spend reading books about counseling— including those in this series (although the purpose of these commentaries is to return the counselor's focus to the Bible).

II Timothy 2

16 But avoid irreligious chatter, because it will lead to even more ungodliness,
17 and their talk will eat its way like gangrene. Included among them are Hymenaeus and Philetus,
18 who have missed the truth by taking poor aim, saying that the resurrection has already taken place, thus upsetting the faith of some.

Irreligious chatter must be avoided at all costs; the counselor must not allow his counselee to draw him or others into conversations characterized by such talk. It **will lead to even more ungodliness**. How is that? Well, talk that demeans true religion is talk that arouses even more scurrilous words and actions. One thing leads to another, in such talk, until, the first thing you know, you find yourself either denying truth you hold dear, or making light of the same. Don't let counseling sessions get out of your control. Whenever you determine that the conversation is becoming (or is even tending toward becoming) out of line, draw it to a halt quickly before it leads to **even more ungodliness.**

Talk by persons like those referred to in verse 17 will eat its way through a life or a congregation like gangrene. Paul probably looked across his cell for this example. It is deadly to spiritual life. Be careful, therefore, in allowing the counselee to freely express himself on any subject in any manner. There is nothing Christian about such counseling even though it is commonly advised by others. And, there are Christians who have bought into the practice of free expression as well. You must take charge, know where you are going and seek the information that you know you will need (cf. Proverbs 18:15).

Paul, as we saw, actually mentions certain individuals by name. Why? For several reasons. The church must be aware of the danger that these people present if they attempt to influence a congregation or any member in it. He, therefore, marked out, identified them. Often, you will find yourself doing the same. And, also, they often become well-known examples of, reference points for, the sort of thing that you are talking about. Presumably, they had been speculating about the resurrection in heretical ways (see verse 18). They took poor aim at the truth and missed it by a mile. They were telling people that the resurrection had already occurred. This false doctrine had already upset the faith of some and Paul wanted to check its gangrenous spread.

Some might be upset, but the church would continue through it all. It is planted and built upon a solid **foundation.** That is a fact that, when

19 However, God's foundation stands firm, having this seal inscribed on it: "The Lord knows those who belong to Him," and "Let all who name the Lord's Name stand far off from iniquity."

20 Now in a large house there are not only gold and silver containers, but also wood and earthen ones, and some are for honorable uses and others for dishonorable uses.

21 So then, whoever cleanses himself from these will be a container for honorable use, special, useful to the Master, ready for every good deed.

---

things seem to be going in the wrong direction, needs to be mentioned. Or, if it is you who tend to despair because of the upsetting of some of your counselees by teachers or psychiatrists who encourage your counselees to take poor aim, reread the truth again and take heart! Remember what is written on the foundation **seal: "The Lord knows those who belong to Him."** To "know" them as He does is both to love and protect them. He has not forgotten them. Every last one of the elect (those who are His) will eventually come to Him and receive eternal life. That is a great assurance. But, while there is that assurance, quietism is not implied by it. Indeed, on the seal there is also inscribed an exhortation. It says, in effect, If you are God's then show it by the way you divorce yourself from iniquity. God wants His own to be sure not only of their salvation but to demonstrate it to others as well. That is why you can work for nothing less than solutions to problems that honor God's Name. His Name is at stake in all counseling. To name the Lord's Name is to take one's stand for Jesus Christ, the Lord. To associate a life with Him that is characterized by iniquity is incongruous.

Paul now turns to the figure of a house (the idea of the foundation of the church just mentioned may have prompted him to do so). **In a large house** (that is, one whose inhabitants are wealthy) there are all sorts of vessels. But, says Paul, you can classify them in two categories: expensive and valuable ones (**gold, silver**), inexpensive and unimportant (**clay and wood**) ones. And, in keeping with their value, the former are used for decorative (**honorable**) purposes while the others are used for menial purposes. Now, in God's **house** (the church) there are also varieties of vessels (members). If you will **cleanse yourself** from these sins I have been discussing, Paul observes, you will be **a container for honorable use.** You will adorn the gospel of God, considered **useful** to Him, one He can call on at any time to do anything (**ready for every good deed**).

That is an encouraging word. Those who are continually cleansing themselves from the sins and iniquities that are pressed upon them as

II Timothy 2

22 Now flee from youthful desires but pursue righteousness, faithfulness, love, peace with those who call on the Lord from a clean heart.

---

temptations, are more and more able to render good service for their Lord. The one whose life is reclaimed through counseling, therefore, is of greater use in the House of God. But, notice, it is not solving his problems that is the objective. Rather, it is cleansing him as a vessel fit for the Master's use. It is a matter of throwing off the sins that hinder him from serving well. No lesser goal can be entertained either by counselee or counselor.

Speaking now directly to Timothy (v. 22) Paul urges **flee from youthful desires**. You will counsel youths who face the very same temptations Timothy did. You must give them the very same instruction. The way to deal with temptations to sexual sin, ambition, desire for money, etc., is to turn your back on it whenever the temptation arises. You, too, must advise them that, having put these things behind them, they must run like sixty! But, notice, that is not enough. In accord with the biblical put off / put on dynamic, when he **flees** from temptation to indulge in youthful desires, at the same time, one must **pursue** something as well. One never succeeds in putting off sin in a purely negative way; rather, he must replace it with its biblical alternative. And, it can be no halfhearted effort on the counselee's part. The word translated **pursue** means to track and hunt down until one finds what he is seeking. The word oozes with ideas of persistent effort and determination. Notice, when Jesus was tempted, He also turned to the Scriptures to counter the temptation. This is the way to pursue those positive characteristics that must replace the sinful activities that are suggested by the temptation.

But, specifically, what is the youthful counselee to pursue in place of his desires? Paul mentions them in verse 22: **righteousness, faith, love, peace with those who call on the Lord from a clean heart.** These elements are standard terms that Paul employs again and again to describe those things that God, the Spirit, produces in us when we walk by the Spirit (see the Spirit's fruit listed in Galatians 5 and comments made there). It is interesting that though these very elements of successful Christian living are called the Spirit's fruit, they are here described as something that the believer must **pursue**. Obviously, therefore, the way in which the Spirit produces His fruit is not through some passive "yielding" of the believer who then waits for the Spirit to act; no, it is through active, energetic obedience of the Christian to the Spirit's Words in His book, the

Christian Counselor's Commentary

23 But avoid foolish and undisciplined speculations, knowing that they breed battles—

Bible. But, of course, even this activity is energized by the Spirit (Cf. Philippians 2:13) who initiates it (often by convicting us of sin) and who then enables us to fulfill the commands of God. Thus, though the Christian pursues, the final result is called the fruit of the Spirit because even the pursuit is Spirit-driven. This is often difficult for some counselees to comprehend—how the Spirit and they work together. You must explain this cooperative effort to them as best they are able to hear it, but (at all costs) make it clear that they are obligated to obey the commands of the Bible. The Spirit will not do the obeying for them!

Righteousness, etc., are all defined in various parts of the Bible. And, although mentioned here in general terms, are not to be taken only generally. The counselor must help the counselee to determine specifically what the righteous thing is that he must do in his particular situation, what the loving thing is, etc. The way to **peace** with other believers is often one that needs full consideration. Sometimes it takes great patience to sort everything out. Others do not always have clean hearts but, through faith, their hearts are considered cleansed by the sprinkling of the blood of Jesus Christ (I Peter 1:2). It is in that sense that Paul is speaking here, using the phrase as a circumlocution for the word "believer." So you must not let the counselee get off the hook by claiming that he doesn't have to be at peace with other believers unless they are perfectly sanctified. This phrase means *every* believer (You may wish to cross-reference him to Romans 12:18 in this regard).

Again, it is the sort of argumentativeness that is characteristic of many false teachers that Timothy must avoid. As a counselor, while clearly making a biblical case for what you are saying, you must stop short of useless argumentation that **breeds battles.** In particular, those speculative ideas and suggestions with which counselees may wish to waste valuable counseling time must be avoided. Don't even get involved in them. Notice, for instance, the way in which the woman at the well jumps to a theological dispute when Jesus puts the finger on her sin. What does Jesus do? In one word he deals with the theological issue and then returns immediately to the main issue—the woman's need of a Savior. This is the thing to do. Don't allow counselees to sidetrack you when you are zeroing in on their sin. Watch out for the tendency.

Such **foolish and undisciplined speculations** (about matters not

II Timothy 2

24 and the Lord's slave must not fight, but rather must be gentle toward everyone, teachable, tolerant,
25 in meekness correcting those who oppose, in hope that God may bring them by repentance into the full knowledge of the truth,

---

mentioned in the Bible) to which Deuteronomy 29:29 probably refers, are not for your counselees to figure out. Point out to them that these things belong to God if He has not revealed them in the Bible. To speculate about them, then, is nothing less than an attempt to steal from God what He has clearly said belongs to Him. Put this way most counselees will back off. Your counselee needs to pay attention to those things that have been "revealed" and *are* pertinent to his situation.

An additional reason for you to refrain from such speculative discussions that go on and on breeding more and more of the same, is because the Lord's ministers **must not fight**. The Lord Himself refused to do so, and His servants must not either. They must not be rude or rough toward counselees, but gentle—toward them all. Even to those who want to do all the wrong things. It is not your task to punish anyone; you must leave that to the Lord. But gentleness does not mean giving in to wrong courses of action, discussion or thought that they may wish to introduce into counseling. There must be a firmness in the gentleness that, as you doubtless have found, is a balance difficult to attain. You must always work toward achieving that kind of approach, walking on the knife's edge, but never falling off on the one side or the other.

Your method is **teaching** (and, as the word could be translated, **being teachable**). Both attributes must be true of the competent counselor. He must always be willing to learn—even from counselees and from counseling sessions (indeed, at the end of every case he ought to have learned something new) in ways that will enrich his own teaching. And, as I have frequently observed, teaching is important in counseling. Contrary to Rogerianism, that assumes knowledge in the counselee that must only be retrieved, biblical counseling recognizes man's need for instruction from the Word of God. One of your principal tasks, therefore, is to teach counselees what God's Word has to say about their problems and how He intends for them to solve these problems in a godly manner.

The counselor, therefore, does not refrain from **correcting** those counselees who are in error; indeed, that is precisely what he must do (v. 25). But he must do so **meekly**. His goal must always be to present biblical truth so that counselees may be brought to **repentance** if God sees fit

Christian Counselor's Commentary

> 26 and that they may come to their senses and escape from the devil's trap—having been captured by him—to do His will.

to use His Word to do so. This goes for unbelievers and for believers alike. Counseling always presupposes need for repentance that leads to eternal life as the goal for talking to unbelievers and, whenever necessary, repentance that grows out of eternal life for talking to Christians.

Here, it seems that these, who had gone so far, were saints—in grave error. The objective, then, was to see them regain their senses, escape from the Devil's trap into which they had fallen, and whose policies (as a result) they were furthering unwittingly. Paul is a generous man who will work with people who have fallen far down. He will not give up on them. He will work as long as there appears to be even the slightest hope. Counselors must take a leaf from his book.

Chapter 3

1 But take note of this: in the last days difficult times will set in.
2 People will be self-centered, money-seekers, braggers, arrogant, blasphemers, disobedient to parents ungrateful, unholy,

---

Paul now looks forward again. He sees in these **last days** of the old order perilous times that, like a thick fog will **settle in** on the church. He wants Timothy to be aware that it is coming. There should be no surprises. Ministry will be **difficult** in times like these, but he must continue. Perhaps the most difficult aspect of ministry in **difficult times** is staying true. After describing, in great detail, precisely what to expect, he spends the remaining portion of the chapter telling Timothy how to continue true and faithful to God. The times, as Paul describes them, are similar to times that we currently experience. Therefore, what Paul says is quite important.

Self-centeredness is the first item on Paul's list, and perhaps what he considered the fountainhead of all that follows. The emphasis on self encountered in so many counseling books today is evidence of the failure of our society. By the fact that it is picked up, packaged and propagated even by Christian authors is also evidence of serious failure in the church. This trend, like all other false counseling dogmas that from time to time seep into the thinking and life of many Christians, will run its course, only to be replaced by other false views. But, at the present time, hardly a book can be cracked that doesn't mention self-love, self-esteem or self-worth. All these concepts, promulgated in the church as well as outside of it, are evidence of the fact that, once again, difficult times are beginning to set in.

Those who exalt self see no reason why they shouldn't be paid very generously, even when they have offered nothing to merit it. They are **money-seekers**. For the best commentary on this problem, see I Timothy, chapter 6. Many counselees are in trouble because they live for money.

Braggers, those who are arrogant, blasphemers, disobedient to parents, ungrateful, unholy, will all wend their way into your counseling room. These patterns of life must be identified (in biblical labels—and this chapter is a great place from which to obtain biblical labels for human sinful behavior) for what they are and dealt with summarily. Sometimes, the thing to do is to read this list from II Timothy and ask, "Can you iden-

> 3 heartless toward family members, merciless, slanderers, uncontrolled, untamed, haters of good,

tify any traits of your life here?" That will often occasion a fruitful discussion. Ours is a day of sheer **arrogance**. People seem to have virtually no respect for God and exercise little humility in the presence of rightful authority. We live in an in-your-face society. They arrogantly brag about their so-called value and worth in which, unfortunately, they have been taught to believe.

In unbelievable ways, God is **blasphemed** (spoken ill of or made fun of). Simply review some of the National Endowment for the Arts presentations, if you need examples. How many times do you have problems with children who are **disobedient to their parents**? Probably these are as numerous as any other counseling problems you face. Who, today, is grateful to God? Or even to others? There is a host of ungrateful Christians who are complainers; people who because of their emphasis on self, think they deserve more than they get. Such people need to be confronted about their ingratitude. No Christian has anything to say to God but a humble and contrite "thank you." He deserves nothing, but has received so much. Tell the whining, ungrateful Christian so in no uncertain terms. He needs to be reminded that all he has or is that is worthwhile is the result of God's good grace. **Unholy** Christians are those who have identified closely with the world. In no way can you see in their lives that they are saints ("set apart ones"). There ought to be something different about the language and life of the believer. He ought to be distinguishable from the unbeliever.

Verse three goes on relentlessly describing the sins of the period in which Timothy (and you) must minister. People are **heartless**. Look at the murders, rapes, vicious crimes that are committed without remorse. They are **merciless, slanderers, uncontrolled, untamed, haters of good.** How descriptive of the people that you meet every day today! Where is the **mercy** shown to those in need? Even among Christians, in many instances, it is lacking. **Slander** characterizes what one may expect in many churches today. And, for sure, it is a part of many counseling rooms. You must not allow slander to take place in counseling sessions. If someone is talking about another behind his back, stop him and warn him of the danger of falling into the sin of slander. There are some Christians who do little more than vilify others. They have little or nothing constructive to write or say; they simply spend their time digging for dirt and trot-

4 informers, impertinent, conceited, pleasure-centered rather than God-centered,

---

ting it out before others. I'm not talking about the necessary and helpful exposure of error that, left unexposed, may harm the members of Christ's church. Indeed, it is often those who expose such error (as Paul regularly did) who are themselves slandered *as slanderers*! There is danger on both sides here. And, to boot, one must be sure of his motives as well as the way in which he handles hot truth.

Those labeled **untamed, uncontrolled**, are those who do what they think is right in their own eyes. They do not recognize legitimate authority, they fail to set a righteous course for themselves; rather, they do as they please, according to their whims. They interpret an ordered life, devoid of self-determination as knuckling under. And they will have nothing of it. They call commandments of Scripture legalistic when you refer to them. They do not wish to acknowledge a difference between rightful exercise of law and legalism. Many Christians live a freewheeling life in which they refuse to join a church and come under its care and discipline. They want no authority above themselves. Thereby, unknowingly, they throw off God's own authority as if it were a burdensome yoke. Part of your task is to persuade such Christians from the Bible that failure to heed God's discipline in a church is disobedience. **Haters of good** characterize every society that calls good evil and evil good. Would you say that we live in such a society? What, then, would God have you as a counselor to do about it as it affects God's people?

But Paul has not finished his devastatingly accurate portrayal of sinful men on the loose. In verse 4 he continues, calling people **informers, impertinent persons, those clouded with pride, pleasure-centered rather than God-centered**. These additions round off a most impressive list of insights into human sin. Study them all—they are the people with whom you are working.

The word **Informers** presuppose a time of persecution in which one person turns in another to the authorities. Children are doing this to parents today, calling them abusers, etc., even when it is not true. And the society in which we live not only condones such behavior but teaches and encourages it. While not yet widespread, persecution toward those who practice Christian values (spanking, Christian education) is already beginning to be felt. In times ahead, unless God does a marvelous work of changing our land, you will be counseling (perhaps underground) people

5 having a form of godliness, but rejecting its power. Also turn away from such people.
6 From among people like these are those who worm their way into houses and capture weak women who are loaded with sins and led by all sorts of desires,
7 who are always learning and never able to come to a full knowledge of the truth.

---

in persecution. Much of what has been said already in this letter is pertinent to those who will suffer.

Impertinent people abound. How do they get that way? They are **clouded with pride** so that they do not recognize their words and behavior for what it is. And in their pursuit of **pleasure** (the national religion of America, symbolized especially by the focus on TV and sports), they are centered on what pleases themselves rather than what pleases God. These things are true not only of unbelievers, but, insofar as they have been affected by the world, of believers as well. That is why you will counsel people with every one of these characteristics. Not all will have all, but there will be combinations of several of these traits in most of the persons that you counsel. And, as times get worse, the problems these difficulties raise for counselors will multiply. You need to be prepared to deal with them in ever-increasing numbers.

The people here described may have an outward **form of godliness** (they go through the rituals) but within there is nothing but a shriveled up soul. True godliness has power to overcome sin and iniquity. Why do Christians fall for the world's sins so often? Because they too have so little power to withstand. That means so little godliness within. It is, therefore, necessary for you to encourage your counselees to become godly (i.e., persons influenced more and more by God). Then, they will experience power over temptation, no matter how difficult their times and their individual circumstances may be. From the influence of such unbelieving persons Paul says, **turn away** (cf. I Corinthians 15:33). Stop letting them ruin you and your lifestyle.

What is the problem with such people? Not simply their sinful lifestyles. But they are bound to do damage to the Church of Christ if their efforts are not resisted (cf. vv. 6, 7). They find ways to **worm their way into the houses of women who are weak** because of their many **sins**. Vulnerable women lead lives not charted by the Spirit in the Word, but driven by **all sorts of** [sinful] **desires**. Those two things are always, in the Scriptures, set over against one another. These desires are the desires of

II Timothy 3

8 Just as Jannes and Jambres opposed Moses, so also these people oppose the truth; they are persons with corrupted minds, rejects when it comes to the faith.

9 But they won't get much farther, because the folly of these people will be as plain to everyone as theirs also became.

10 You, in contrast, as my disciple, have closely followed my teaching, my way of life, my purpose, my faith, my patience, my love, my endurance,

---

the flesh—the body wrongly habituated in sinful ways by the sinful nature with which we all were born. These women are intrigued by **all sorts of learning** (presumably, the false teachers worm their way in by offering new teachings) but fail to accept the **truth**.

Now, Paul names others, from Old Testament times, who provide an example of the sort of disrespect these people have for God, His authority, and His **truth**. Among them is not only an inability to find truth, but whenever they encounter it, they **oppose** it. These unsaved teachers are **rejects** (those who have had to be put out of the church) when it comes to exhibiting Christian **faith**. Their **minds** have been **corrupted** by sin, so they do not see the truth. But, Paul is encouraged, God will let them get only so far before their **folly** is recognized by the members of the Church—just as the folly of Jannes and Jambres was. That is the confidence that we may have: God will not let His church become entirely perverted. There will be a point, in every difficult time, when some will recognize the folly with which the church has been affected and reform it. Today, we need a reformation in counseling in the church.

Coming to verse 10, after this most realistic and possibly disheartening picture of the times that are ahead, Paul makes it abundantly clear to Timothy that he need not succumb to the temptations that it will bring with it. He can carry on after Paul's demise successfully. Why does he think this is possible? Because Timothy has seen heard, participated and thought in the very ways that Paul had. If Paul could do it (and he did) so could Timothy. So, in verses 10, 11, Paul reiterates the ways in which Timothy had experienced, along with him as his constant companion, what he would need to endure difficult times. In contrast to those who were falling into the temptations of the times, Timothy had **closely followed** Paul's teaching. That is, he knew not only what Paul taught, but had received a form of teaching by which he could preserve not just its substance but also its presentation. He knew all about it.

I remember traveling with two other persons during a summer in

Christian Counselor's Commentary

11 my persecutions, and the sufferings that I underwent at Antioch, at Iconium and at Lystra, what persecutions I bore. But the Lord rescued me from all of them.

---

which we preached time and again, often the same messages in different places. We became so familiar with each other's talks that we jokingly said "I think we could switch messages and preach each other's sermons as well as the one who composed them." We never actually did so, but it would have been possible, I am convinced. Something like this happened to Timothy; he could deliver Paul's messages, counsel as Paul counseled, work with people in forming and strengthening churches as Paul did because he had so **closely followed** him in all aspects of the ministry. That is the way to train ministers and, in particular, to train them in counseling. Timothy knew Paul's **way of life:** how he handled himself before God and men. He knew what made a man a good minister of the Word. He knew his **purpose**—what he wanted his life to count for; what he planned to do in the spreading of the message around the Mediterranean world, and other goals and objectives he held dear. He had closely followed Paul's **faith**; how he was able to trust God in every sort of situation, and how God had blessed that faith. He saw Paul's **patience** with people, in face of setbacks, when he was persecuted. He experienced Paul's **love** toward himself, toward others and, most importantly, toward the Lord Jesus Christ. He had seen Paul **endure** suffering. He especially could remember (as Paul mentions it) what happened at **Antioch, at Iconium and at Lystra.** Timothy knew about all of these extraordinary times of suffering—especially at Lystra, Timothy's home town—where Paul was left in a pile of stones for dead. But, Paul reminds Timothy, **the Lord rescued me from all of them.** That is the point: if you know that God will rescue you, you can endure anything (cf. I Corinthians 10:13).

Now, what is the larger point in all of this? Whether he knew it or not, Timothy was ready and prepared for the ministry that Paul was handing over to him. Timothy might not have thought so, and he might not have realized that all of these events he experienced with Paul was a part of God's providential training. Paul is now explaining that fact to him. Perhaps one of the most important things that a counselor can learn in training others is to let them experience many counseling cases with him. The best training is discipleship. That's how the Lord trained His disciples, that is how Paul trained Timothy, and if you want to train others, take them into counseling sessions with you. For many years at C.C.E.F. we

II Timothy 3

12 In fact, all who want to live a godly life for Christ Jesus will be persecuted.
13 Evil persons and imposters will go on to their worst, deceiving and being deceived.

---

trained at least two men in every case. Not only was it helpful to them, but also to the trainer as well. After the case, we could discuss its various aspects. In these discussions many important insights that might have been lost on one person alone were voiced. The counselor is also kept on his mettle; he cannot afford to get sloppy in front of others he is trying to train. If you have never done this before, why not turn an elder or deacon into a Timothy?

As a side comment, in verse 12 Paul makes a statement that many counselees (and counselors, for that matter) don't like to hear: **All who want to live a godly life in Christ Jesus will be persecuted.** Take that to heart. If you have never suffered for your faith, consider why. Either you are not living a godly enough life to bring persecution on yourself or it just hasn't hit yet. But the statement seems to be an absolute. Don't get discouraged, Timothy (counselee) if you are persecuted because you are living as a Christian should; *expect* it. And, in this proposition he is telling Timothy, even if you were not to take up this ministry, you would not avoid persecution thereby.

Things are not going to get better—even in the Church (v. 13). **Evil persons and imposters** (people who are out to deceive) will not grow less in numbers and their influence will not abate. In fact, they will increase in number and influence, **deceiving others and being deceived.** That means, as Paul is quick to point out, things will go on in this manner until they reach their **worst**. Not a pretty picture, but realistic. Paul was not a cynical old man; he was utterly realistic. And that is exactly what you must be when working with counselees. Don't paint unrealistic, rose-colored pictures of what Christian counseling can magically do. Tell counselees that it will mean hard work, that there will be many obstacles in the way, that there will be people who will oppose (and who, in addition to criticizing, will offer unbiblical solutions to problems) as well as those difficult, new ways that they must learn. Let people know what is involved. But, at the same time, make it clear that God will enable them to do all that is necessary if only they will mean business with Him. What you should offer is realism and encouragement in proper proportions. Size up what the counselee needs most (encouragement or a dose of realism)

Christian Counselor's Commentary

14 You, however, must continue in those things that you learned and are convinced of, knowing from whom you learned them,
15 and that from childhood you have known the sacred Scriptures, that are able to make you wise about salvation through faith in Christ Jesus.

---

and, while administering both to him, do so in proportion to his need.

And, as verse 12 indicates, it is often very unrealistic to imagine that things will get better, that people will improve. Never count on this. Things may get far worse; indeed, at times (as Paul says) they will reach their **worst**!. Prepare your counselee for the worst (as Paul does) and he will be able not only to handle this God's way, but anything lesser that may come his way. If he can handle the worst; he can handle the not - quite- so- bad as well.

Now, Paul focuses on what it is that will get Timothy through the worst of times. **You**, he says (in contrast to others who might not do so) **must continue in those things that you learned and are convinced of, knowing from whom you learned them** (v. 14). When the winds of adversity, apostasy and heresy are blowing their hardest, when the tips of the palm trees are touching the ground and tiles are flying off the roof, when the values of a stable society have not only been blown away, but are replaced by iniquitous anarchistic alternatives (such as those listed in the first eight verses of this chapter), there is a place to turn that will keep you rooted and grounded in the truth. It is a place where you will find all you need to stay true when all else seems up for grabs. That place is in the Scriptures. In verse 14, Paul speaks of the apostolic message that Timothy heard from him. That message, today, is found only one place—in the New Testament. Today, then, tell your Timothy-like counselees, if they stay close to the Bible, they will stay true to Its Author.

And, he goes on to say, stay with the Old Testament Scriptures that you learned **from childhood** (v. 15). These Scriptures are able to make one **wise about salvation through faith in Christ.** But they will do far more for you once you have exercised faith and experienced that salvation. The Bible is all you need to preach the gospel, and as I shall show you now, all that you need for your entire ministry to believers.

The next two verses are so important for counselors that I have written an entire book, *How to Help People Change, based* on the facts taught therein. Because of that, I shall note briefly but a few elements in the passage.

All Scripture is inspired by God, says Paul. In this regard, note that

II Timothy 3

16 All Scripture is breathed out by God and useful for teaching, for conviction, for correction and for disciplined training in righteousness,

---

it is not the writers of the Bible who are inspired, but the writings that they produced. The word "inspired" is a compound term that ought to read **"breathed out by God."** What Paul is affirming about the Bible is that it is as much the very word of God *as if* it had been spoken audibly by God by means of breath. It is His *Word*. If God were to speak audibly what He wants us to know, He would say nothing more, nothing less and nothing different than what He has written in It. It is identical with anything He might have spoken by breath.

Because that is true, the Bible is unique. It is inerrant. It can be trusted implicitly; you can know that its statements are true and that its warnings and promises are sure. And, of importance here, is that it is a **useful** Book. In it you can find all the **teaching** that is necessary to know God's will. It teaches all things necessary for life and godliness. What God wants each one to know about faith (what he should believe) and life (what he should do) may be found here. It is an absolute standard, given by God for human living.

Secondly, the Bible not only tells us what God requires of us, it goes on to **convict** us of our failures to fulfill those requirements. The word convict is a court term that means to so prosecute the case against one that he is declared guilty of the crime of which he is accused. In counseling it is not only necessary to be able to show your counselee what God requires of him from the Bible, but also to show him from the same Source that he stands condemned when he fails to meet those requirements.

But the Bible does not leave you there—condemned. If you continue with it, It will show you how to get out of the mess you got yourself into. It will teach you how to seek forgiveness from God and men through genuine repentance. The third thing that it does for you, then, is **correct** you. Literally, the word means "to stand up straight again." If the Bible convicts you of sin (knocks you flat on your face) It also picks you up, dusts you off, gets you out of the trouble you brought on yourself and heads you in the right direction for the future.

But that is still not enough. You will once more fall into the same sins if you do not adopt God's new ways. So, the fourth thing that the Bible does is **discipline you in righteousness**. By godly, biblical discipline you must learn to put off the old sinful ways while replacing them with God's righteous ways.

Christian Counselor's Commentary

17 in order to make the man from God adequate, and to equip him fully for every good task.

Now, what are those four things? They are four steps in a process of change. Every counselor is out to change his counselee in some way. Here is how God says that Christian counselors must do so. They must use the Scriptures in the way He has indicated. Now, many counselors who purport to be Christian do nothing of the sort. Are you among them? Well, in the light of these verses don't you recognize that you cannot substitute human methods (the counsel of the ungodly) for those given by God and still call what you are doing Christian counseling—at least, you can't do so with integrity. Get honest! Admit that you are not doing Christian counseling—or start doing it.

"But, can't we bring other ideas into our counseling along with this four-step method that depends on the Bible?" Well, look at verse 17. The Bible is given, Paul says, to change people in these ways. And, he goes on to say, it is **given in order to make the man of God adequate, and equip him fully for every good work**. If your ministry of changing people is biblical, that is all that is necessary. The church didn't have to sit around for 1900+ years waiting for Freud and others to tell Christians how to change people. God has been in the business of doing this since the fall. No, if understood and used properly, the Bible will make you, as a **"man of God"** (a designation picked up from the Old Testament to mean the man—or minister—sent from God) **adequate.** If something is adequate, does it need to be supplemented? Not only does Paul claim that the Bible makes him adequate for his ministry of counseling, but he also says by it he is **fully equipped**. If you are fully equipped, do you need to add something more? And, finally, he says, the man of God, depending on the Scriptures alone, is ready to perform **every good task** to which God calls him. Doesn't look like he needs more, does it? Jesus, using the Old Testament alone, was able to counsel *perfectly.* The problem is not with the Bible, but with those who do not know it well-enough. Christians have spent more time studying books written by unbelievers (or by Christians who, themselves, propagate their views} than they have studying the Bible. That is the reason for this set of commentaries—to encourage Christian counselors to think more fully about what they can learn concerning principles and practices of counseling from the Bible Itself.

CHAPTER 4

1 In the presence of God and of Jesus Christ, Who is going to judge the living and the dead, and by His appearing and His empire, I solemnly call on you to

---

In the 22 verses remaining in this letter we have what are the last recorded words of Paul. They are filled with interest not only about the man, exhibiting both pathos and victory, but also about matters pertaining, one way or another, to counseling. It is a solemn moment for Paul as he thinks of closing this letter to his dear friend and child in the faith. He so wants Timothy to follow in his footsteps that he continues to enforce point after point by way of exhortation, directions and warning. Indeed, he goes further. He bids Timothy to take an oath to **preach the Word at all times**, in a manner that is consonant with the ministry that he is inheriting (vv. 1, 2). Calling on Timothy to acknowledge God's **presence** as both Father and Son (an oath is a calling on God to witness what one promises to do), Paul **solemnly** urges Timothy to **preach the Word in season and out of season.** To enforce the importance of the oath as he inducts him into the ministry he is handing over to him, he emphasizes that God is going to **judge the living and the dead**. And, he adds, I urge you to take the oath in His presence and **by His appearing and empire**. It is a definitive moment for the great apostle. He knows his own ministry is finished; he wants Timothy to pick it up and faithfully carry it forth. It is to him above all others that Paul assigns it. That is why it begins with an oath, replete with the warning that God is watching and that He will judge whether Timothy will accept the office and fulfill it to the full.

There are times to call on counselees to solemnly declare their purposes. Indecision, hesitation, lagging behind when they should be going forward, are all times to consider issuing a solemn challenge (I do not necessarily suggest that it take the form of an oath, although there may be some situations in which nothing less would do). Timothy was hesitant to assume the place Paul was offering him; Paul, therefore, by urging an oath upon him, was calling for a decision that, because of its solemn nature, would irrevocably commit him to it.

What is it that Timothy is to do in this ministry? What Paul did—**preach the Word** (or message) when people were happy to hear it, and even when they were not. What people thought was unimportant; what

Christian Counselor's Commentary

> 2 preach the Word, be at it in season and out of season. Convict, reprove, urge with complete patience and full teaching.

God thought was all-important. And God wanted His Word proclaimed to every tribe, tongue and nation. Difficult times were ahead, as we have seen in Chapter Three. Preaching the gospel frequently would be out of season. That was no reason to abandon the work. As a counselor, there are times when what you have to say will seem unseasonable to counselees. They will think themselves inconvenienced by it. They will not be at all happy to hear what you say. But they need to hear anyway, **in season or out of season**.

How is it to be preached? By **convicting** people of sin (see 3:16). Don't let anyone tell you that the ministry of the Word that involves conviction of sin is inappropriate to counseling. It is, as we saw in the previous chapter, part of the process of change. Until one is thoroughly convinced that he is sinning, it is unlikely that he will be sufficiently motivated to change. He must recognize that his behavior must be changed not because it is inconvenient or troublesome to himself, but *because it displeases God.* No lesser motive will do.

Moreover, he is to **reprove** those to whom he speaks whenever he recognizes sin in their lives. The kind of preaching that Paul calls for in this verse is seldom heard today. Perhaps it is heard even less in the ministry of the Word in counseling. The unbiblical idea of acceptance has so permeated the counseling field that Christians are reluctant to convict of sin and reprove others. It just isn't done! Well, maybe not, but it ought to be. That is what Paul tells Timothy—and you.

And Timothy is to **urge** people to believe and follow the teachings of God's Word. Like it or not, that means putting pressure on them. Paul was not loathe to do that very thing. In this letter in which he is counseling Timothy, he puts extraordinary pressure on him. At every turn he is urging him to accept and carry on the ministry he is leaving behind. Take a look at Philemon sometime and notice the unusual amount of pressure (urging) of various sorts that Paul exerts on the recipient of that letter! A minister of the Word has authority, and there are times to exert it. Authority and pressure can be improperly brought to bear on others, that is true, but follow Paul in doing so and you will not go wrong. It would be to your benefit, and the benefit of your counselees, to make a study of the ways and means that the apostles legitimately urged others to do God's will. Counseling involves much urging. Certainly, the apostles did not simply

II Timothy 4

3 A time is coming when they won't put up with healthy teaching, but rather, because they want their ears scratched, they will heap up teachers who are in keeping with their own desires.
4 And (on the one hand) they will turn away from the truth while (on the other) they will turn aside to myths.

---

explain matters and leave it to the counselee to take it from there. The word translated urge can mean persuade; but, basically, it means to use all legitimate means available to assist another in fulfilling a biblical command.

Note carefully the qualification, **with all patience and full teaching**. You are to convict and urge, but not in a way that fails to take into consideration that people may have reasons for refusing to do what you think they should. Exhibiting patience to ferret out those reasons, to answer each one biblically, and finally convince the counselee of God's will, often is necessary. And, one of those reasons—a legitimate one—is that the person does not know how to do what the Bible exhorts him to do. Therefore, he must first be **taught**. Until the counselee fully knows not only what to do but also how to pull it off, he may not be ready to act. You are to be a patient teacher in such instances, just as Paul was with Timothy to whom he showed infinite patience.

That out of season time when people **will not put up with healthy teaching**, Paul says, is approaching. Being a prophet he may have known this by revelation. Perhaps he was merely reading the signs of the times. Either way, he is warning Timothy that there would be rough days ahead for preachers of the truth. False **teachers**, on the other hand, would have a heyday (v. 3). People will **heap up** such teachers because they **scratch their itching ears** and teach things that are in accord with their sinful **desires**. Sound like our day? Sound like the things that some of the advocates of church growth teach? Sound like the sociological norms that are set forth in such programs? Think about it. More to the point—does it sound like the sort of thing many encourage you to do in counseling?

Such self-serving counselees **turn away from the truth**; but they do not simply reject something. At the same time **they turn aside to myths**. I could expatiate on the myths of psychotherapeutic counseling till the cows come home, but because I have written so much in that vein, I will refrain. I simply want to point out that those who turn from biblical counseling turn to **myths**. Let me ask you, how many myths about counselees and principles of counseling have you swallowed? They are afloat every-

Christian Counselor's Commentary

5 But you, be levelheaded in all of it, endure hardship, do the work of an evangelist, carry out your service to the full.

6 As for me, I am already being poured out like a drink offering, and the time for my departure has arrived.

7 I have fought the gallant fight, I have finished the race, I have kept the faith.

---

where in Christian circles just as they are in non-Christian ones. Can you distinguish between what is myth and what is not? If you can't your counseling, I warn you, is probably shot-through with them. Check it out—shouldn't you?

You are to be **levelheaded** enough to know the difference between truth and myth and not be swayed by every new idea that is cast up on the shore (v. 5). Moreover, you are to win people to Christ whenever the occasion to do so arises. Those unbelievers who come for counseling need to be evangelized. At the point at which you recognize that the person seeking counsel is not a Christian, your role as counselor changes to the role of an **evangelist**.

You have a ministry that God expects you to carry out to the full. You cannot say "I'm only a counselor; I don't evangelize." All ministry for Christ involves evangelism as well as edification. You must be ready and willing to carry out every aspect of that ministry or you will not be a faithful servant of Jesus Christ.

Now Paul is thinking of closing. He knows his ministry is over: **As for me, I am already being poured out like a drink offering, and the time for my departure has arrived** (v. 6). He pictures his life as a willingly-given sacrifice to God; a drink offering. There is evidence that he will not escape the clutches of Nero the second time. He is going to be put to death. Notice how he describes death: **my departure**. Paul sees himself setting sail for a new land. For the Christian, death is leaving this country for another, a heavenly one. You will counsel Christians with terminal illnesses. To think of death with them in these terms is very helpful because it is to the point. Paul's focus is not on the grave but on the place to which his spirit will travel. He is going to be **with Christ, which is far better** than anything here and now.

But, as you speak, you may also turn to the next verse. Here Paul looks back and sees the implications of his life for the future. He writes, **I have fought the good fight, I have finished the race, I have kept the faith** (v. 7). That is a remarkable statement. Not that Paul meant he had

II Timothy 4

8   What is left for me is the winner's wreath of righteousness lying at a distance, that the Lord, (Who is the righteous Judge) will award to me on that Day; and not to me alone but also to all those who have loved His appearing.
9 Do your best to come to me soon;
10   Demas has deserted me because he loved the present age, and went off to Thessalonica; Crescens has gone to Galatia, Titus to Dalmatia.

---

been perfect; indeed, elsewhere he calls himself the chief of sinners. But he had accomplished what God called him to do. He had overcome the enemy as he battled for the truth (he did not succumb to false teaching, threats, persecution), he crossed the finish line without giving up the race somewhere along the track; in short, he had been faithful. This he says not to boast but because he wants Timothy to see that it is possible, and for him to **closely follow** his example in this as well. To those staring death in the face, you may ask, "Even at this late date, is there still more to do? Or have you completed the race? Are there others to whom you ought to speak words of encouragement from the course of your life? Either positively or negatively? Is this not an important time to take your young Timothys in hand and speak words of lasting import to them?" You can be sure that Timothy treasured this letter. Would someone treasure one from you?

What is **left** for Paul? Nothing in this life. He looks forward to receiving the prize of the **winner's wreath** that still **lies at a distance** in that other land toward which he is now to travel. There, the **Lord Jesus, Who is a righteous Judge** (unlike so many others in this world) will award the wreath to Paul **in that Day** when he sees Him face to face. But, Paul hastens to add, this hope is not for me alone, but it should be the glorious expectation of **all those who [in this life] have loved His appearing.** There is much to look forward to in Christ. Make the most of these things with dying counselees—or with those grieving over loved ones who have died.

Now for some final comments, all of which are not necessarily connected. They comprise matters that Paul wants not to fail mentioning at the close of the letter. **Come to me soon,** he urges. Make every effort to do so. If Timothy did not come soon, it might be too late. There are times to drop everything, putting other things on hold, to accomplish the one thing most important. Timothy must have read this appeal in that way. Listen to the pathos in the background of the next 4 verses (as you read them, you can hardly blame Paul for wanting to see Timothy). Demas has

Christian Counselor's Commentary

11 Luke alone is with me. Get Mark and bring him along with you since he is useful in serving me.
12 I sent Tychicus to Ephesus.
13 When you come, bring the traveling cloak that I left with Carpus at Troas, and the scrolls (especially the parchments).
  14 Alexander the coppersmith did many evil things to me; the Lord will repay him in a manner that is in keeping with his deeds.
15 You also must be on guard against him, since he opposed our message.
  16 At my defense nobody stood by me; instead, everybody deserted me. (May it not be counted against them!)

---

deserted Paul, because, contrary to all that motivated the great Apostle, he loved the present age more than the one to come. Shortsighted as he was, Demas turned aside. Others were on important trips and so couldn't be with him. Only Luke was there with him. Mark, who had deserted years before has repented and Paul wants to see him too. He knows how useful he could be. And, Timothy, when you come, bring the heavy, **traveling cloak I left at Troas along with the scrolls—especially the parchments** (his Hebrew Old Testament?). **Winter** is coming on (v. 21); it is cold in the unheated prison. There is nothing to read. I am going to be with the Lord soon, but it is never too late to learn more of him—even now—so bring my books to me. What a preacher, studying to the very end! Much pathos in those words. There is little left for Paul in this world; everything in him is oriented toward the world to come. Yet, he will use whatever time is left profitably, studying, conducting a ministry far and wide through his co-workers. Paul shows us how to leave this world, if anyone ever did. Study these closing verses closely. They afford much help for counseling people who are dealing with death.

A warning—watch out for **Alexander the coppersmith [who] did many evil things to me** (the original possibly indicates it was he whose activities led to Paul's second imprisonment). **Guard against him.** He is a real foe of the gospel, and will probably try to oppose you if he has an opportunity. There are people like this against whom you must warn your counselees, and take warning yourself. You must take precautions to keep their invidious influence from destroying your work: **guard against them**. But Paul is not vindictive. In strict accord with his words in Romans 12 about the Lord avenging evil people, he leaves Alexander to the Lord to deal with.

When he first appeared before Nero for a preliminary hearing of his case, none of those Christians who were in Rome **stood with** him (doubt-

II Timothy 4

17 But the Lord stood with me and strengthened me so that through me the proclamation might be fully preached and all the Gentiles might hear it. And I was rescued from the lion's mouth.
18 The Lord will rescue me from every wicked act and will save me for His heavenly empire. To Him be glory forever and ever! Amen.
19 Greet Prisca and Aquila and the household on Onesiphorus.
20 Erastus remained at Corinth, but I left Trophimus sick at Miletus.
21 Do your best to come before winter. Eubulus greets you along with Pudens and Linus and Claudia and all of the brothers.

---

less, some of those who remained faithful were away on missions). All the locals **deserted** him (but, he hopes that the Lord will not count it against them). Yet, he had all the support one could need: **the Lord stood with him**! If the Lord is there, lending encouragement and support, who else is needed? To Counselees who feel like Elijah or who truly have been deserted in their hour of need, read these great words. They are some of the most comforting and encouraging words in the Bible.

The Lord also **strengthened him** in that hour so that he could preach the gospel to those at the court of Caesar. The gospel had now been taken throughout the **gentile** world, and had even been taught in the palace to the emperor and those around him. At the first hearing, Paul was **rescued from the lion's mouth.** Nero did not at that time sentence him to death. But, something had happened since then. Paul had had at least one more hearing (perhaps a trial itself) at which he was condemned. Even at this late date, when facing death, he sees that God will still deliver him from others who would wrong him (v. 18) and praises Him for it. Christ will preserve him till he reaches the heavenly kingdom. What significant words with which to receive the baton from Paul!

Final greetings to a number of the faithful outside Rome with whom Paul was still in full communion (vv. 19, 20) A final plea: **Do your best to come before winter**. It's already getting cold here. There are some who have either arrived recently (after the first hearing) or who have repented. He is not now alone (v. 21[b]). May God be with you, Timothy, and give you all the help (grace) you need.

That is Paul's last letter. It is one of a kind. There is nothing else like it in the Old or New Testaments. Turn to it often when thinking of death—yours or that of a counselee or his loved one. It is, as you have seen, loaded with help. Moreover, there is nothing else quite like it in terms of handing over one's work to his successor. Pastors who must give up a church, people who, after long years at it must resign from a job, and oth-

Christian Counselor's Commentary

22 The Lord be with your spirit. May help be with you.

---

ers who, in one way or another must pass on their work to others, can all profit greatly from the many helpful insights this letter affords. Use it frequently for counseling in these more-or-less unusual circumstances.

Introduction to TITUS

Paul's letter to Titus is filled with vital information for Christian Counselors. Its very nature dictates that outcome. It is not, fundamentally, a book on preaching, but a letter to an apostolic assistant about how to order and arrange affairs in newly-spawned congregations. During his whirlwind trip through the island of Crete Paul left behind little knots of new converts that were but the embryos of congregations. Now, Titus was to do the work of a midwife. It was his task to organize these motley groups of Christians into well-functioning churches. That task, directly or indirectly, necessarily required him (and Paul with him) to address many of the problems occasioned by disorder as well as questions about how to live this new thing called "the Christian life." As you can see, in a situation of this nature, he must handle many things that are fundamental to Christian counseling.

One thing interesting to note, as we proceed, is the depth of teaching that Paul gave to a congregation from its inception. Here you can find pristine instruction he thought a group of newly-converted persons should have. In concert with I Thessalonians (another book written under similar conditions, upon which I hope to produce a commentary shortly), Titus providentially provides much of this standard guidance, which, because counselees often must be treated as "babes in Christ," is extremely helpful for counselors. As you become more aware of the value of the book's insights into problems (often anticipated by the experienced counselor Paul) you will find yourself turning again and again to the book not only for help in the counseling session, but also for help in the study when thinking about how to improve your counseling ministry.

So, it is with great joy and anticipation that I venture forth with you into the study of this useful letter, trying, as I said in the introduction to the first volume of this series (The Christian Counselor's Commentary: I Corinthians) to do two things: to understand the text and its direct teaching about counseling (together with their implications), and, how Paul goes about dealing with people. In the I Corinthians commentary, there was much of the latter; there, as you know, Paul was combating error and sin of every sort. In Titus, however, you will find more of the former and less of the latter. Yet, there is how-to in dealing with people. Paul is not addressing counselees, as in I Corinthians, but the one who must deal with them. As a result, my comments will be less inferential, and more direct.

Christian Counselor's Commentary

In the book of Titus one counseling practitioner is talking to another. Yet, in the background there is always the fact that what Paul says, he says not only for Titus' benefit, but (as in I & II Timothy) with the understanding that Titus might have to show the letter to the converts with whom he is working. Calvin, many years ago, pointed out this fact about the pastoral letters. As a result, while the letter contains shop talk, there is less than you might expect. It is written with the consciousness that from place to place, others may be reading over Titus' shoulder. The book of apostolic instruction, therefore, could be used by Titus to bolster his work.

Fundamentally, as I said, Titus should not be viewed as a book that has to do with how to preach. Though there are many useful implications for preaching that, doubtless, you may glean from it, mainly, the book concerns what Titus must do in relationship to those people whom Paul left behind, to form them into strong, well-functioning congregations of the Lord Jesus Christ. So, will you read the book with me in this light, asking Paul to tell us too what we need to know about bringing the Word of God to His people in a more powerful way so that they may become people who truly "engage in good deeds[1] (Titus 3:8)?"

---

1. A regularly-stated goal Paul sets forth at the end of each chapter (1:16; 2:14; 3:8, 14). This, significantly, is the ultimate goal of all counseling (cf. Mt. 5:16).

Chapter 1

1 Paul, a slave of God and an apostle of Jesus Christ to promote the faith of God's chosen people and the full knowledge of the truth that is in the interest of godliness

---

The book opens with a recital of the apostolic qualifications of the writer along with the reason why Christ chose him for this task. While truly an "apostle," (one sent forth on a divinely-ordained mission), Paul gladly rejoices in calling himself God's **servant** (literally, "slave"). Although fully exercising apostolic authority (you will hear more about this authority later). Paul refuses to "lord it over" those to whom he ministers. This, in itself, is a sobering thought for counselors. If you and I, who do not have apostolic authority, fail to take a servant attitude in counseling (not to speak of being a slave!), then you can be sure that we are going to fail in the endeavor. Even if God brings about improvement in the lives of your counselees because of His goodness and mercy, that does not necessarily mean that He is pleased with you. So, it is well to catch the tone of the letter from the outset, missing neither the note of authority in the word "apostle," nor the delicately balanced note of humility that identifies you (with Paul) as no more than God's "slave."

Counseling is the work of a slave. A slave has no will of his own; he is to do the will of his master. Those who recognize this and seek to follow God's will, are prepared *in attitude* to counsel biblically. The combination of the two terms, so finely blended in the opening words of the letter, actually helps Paul to assert strong authority. What he says does not originate with him (he is only the slave) but with His Master. It puts the emphasis where it belongs: what you will hear, says Paul, is nothing more or less than God's own Word; obviously, it is not merely the word of a slave. The "apostle" was a "sent off one"—that is, a trusted slave who was appointed by God Himself to carry His message to the world. You too, derivatively, minister under the same commission.

The latter part of the first verse contains two very important statements: first, one about why Paul was appointed an apostle and, secondly, a statement about the effect of truth upon life. Both matters are critical to counselors. God set aside His greatest apostle to "promote the faith of God's chosen people." From eternity past God selected the persons who would comprise His newly formed "chosen people." Some have trouble with election (selection, choosing) because they fail to recognize that He has determined from all eternity not only the end result, but also the means. Paul himself was God's chosen means to bring the Gospel to the nations (Acts 9:15). In the passage in Acts just cited, God calls Paul a "chosen vessel." Clearly, God did not leave the work of gathering together His new people, the church, to happenstance; the details were all worked out beforehand. Yet, this choosing and outworking of the ends and the means was carried on in such a way that those chosen would not receive salvation apart from putting faith in Christ, nor would they be able to do so apart from the faithful preaching of the Word (cf. Romans 10:14-17). At every point, responsibility is maintained.[1]

But Paul was not only chosen to promote faith in God's elect people by preaching the gospel message, he also wanted to teach new converts those things that would fully inform them about the basics of the Christian life. The fact that truth promotes godliness is vital to Christian counselors, since counseling, in brief, is the **promotion of truth among God's people.** And that truth which Paul preached is now embodied in his letters. It is the Word of God (now inscripturated) that Christ said "sanctifies" (John 17:17). Sanctification is the setting apart of one's life more and more from sin to righteousness. That truth, when properly ministered, helps believers to "observe all things" that Christ commanded (Mt. 28:20). That is the process in which Christian counselors are involved.

Now, Paul knew what some counselors have yet to learn: it is truth, and truth alone, that changes counselees in ways that please God. Nothing else, neither the kindness and compassion of the counselor nor the best efforts of the counselee (as important as both may be in their place) will do the job apart from the truth that is necessary to bring about godliness. Neither personality nor techniques will avail. God's truth must be communicated to and received by counselees who do not know it, in order to effect the changes of which God approves. Apart from God's truth, all change is paper thin, a sham that will not stand the pressures of life. It will be tattered to ribbons by the first strong wind that blows. The Holy Spirit "moved" (as Peter put it) the writers of the Scriptures to produce a written Word from God that is available to counselors. Indeed, as Paul implies here, when he speaks of a "full knowledge" of the truth it is a **complete** revelation of God's will, and nothing less, of which he was speaking when he wrote.

---

1. For more on this see my book, *The Grand Demonstration*.

Titus 1

2 that is based on the hope of eternal life that God, Who doesn't lie, promised before time began,

---

Counselors and counselees alike must recognize that the Bible provides all that is necessary for life and godliness. Nothing additional is needed—or should be desired. That it is biblical truth the Holy Spirit uses to transform life as this is communicated, received and acted upon in counseling, means every counselor must have a full knowledge of this truth in order to counsel effectively. That means he must do more than read a few books on counseling, helpful though they may be; he must study his Bible intensively to learn not only what God requires of human beings, but also how to help them bring it off. He must familiarize himself with key passages of Scripture to which he will be able to turn with alacrity and understanding to inform and persuade counselees of God's will. He must understand these passages in such a way that he recognizes their intended impact upon life. To help biblical counselors do just that is the major reason for *The Christian Counselor's Commentary* series. In this verse, for instance, one may prove to a counselee who thinks that a discussion of "doctrine," when counseling is a waste of time, is, instead, most practical to those who wish to learn to live a godly life. And, it may be of use in convincing counselees that superficial (rather than full) knowledge of God's truth, in some cases, may be the very reason for their sinful lifestyles.

Verse two continues the discussion of godliness. Paul says that godliness is based on the hope (in the Bible hope means "expectation," anticipation of something that is certain because God promised it[1]) of eternal life. Godliness is important because this life is not all there is. What is done here counts for all eternity. Godliness is based on that anticipation (cf. I Jn. 3:3). Counselees who have become cynical and wonder whether there is any reason to continue the struggle should be reminded of the fact that, like it or not, life **will** go on—if not here, then, in eternity. And, he assures them that the promise of eternal life that God made to them when they trusted Christ as Savior, most certainly will be kept since God doesn't lie. That promise was made, not in time, but "before time began." That is, before creation. The idea of granting eternal life to those

---

1. It has none of the connotations of our current use of the word to mean a "hope-so" hope. The "blessed hope" (mentioned in Titus 2:13) is *not* the blessed hope-so!

Christian Counselor's Commentary

3   and at just the right time has been made plain by the preaching with which I have been entrusted by the order of God our Savior;

---

redeemed by the blood of Jesus Christ was not an afterthought, but was part of a grand plan God had always determined to effect. It is important for discouraged, disheartened counselees to realize that this life is not the end. And, it is equally important to assure them that difficulties and suffering encountered here are but for a short while and are played out in time for eternal purposes that are glorious and beneficent. (See *The Grand Demonstration, op. cit.,* for details). Perseverance in counseling often may be lacking simply because this important anticipation of the eternal consequences of their present behavior has grown dim. It is often the task of the counselor to revive and brighten it for his counselee.

But, though planned from all eternity, this hope was revealed in time—at just the **right** time (cf. Galatians 4:4; I Timothy 2:6)! God has a timetable by which He is conducting His affairs. And, Paul explains, he was one who was chosen by God to make it known to those who heard his preaching (v. 3). The message he preached, and the preaching he did in Crete and elsewhere, had been entrusted to him by God the Savior's orders (the word "orders" is a military term). Paul was "ordered" by God to do His work; he did not take the ministry upon himself. Again, this introductory section is vitally important to all that follows. What Paul, in turn, is about to order in the churches by the hand of Titus, who was to organize them, again, was all from God. Paul wanted them to know that everything was based on divine authority. Counselors who do not see their work in the same way, lack an essential quality for effective counseling: they lack the authority that ought to lie behind all true ministry. The matter of authoritative orders, that God has issued to His counselors, also is important for counselees. They are not to follow the whims of counselors but the written, certain promises and commands of their Great God and Savior, Jesus Christ. Anything counselors recommend to counselees, they ought to be able to support biblically. In fact, they should inform them as fully as possible about all aspects of the problem and the solution. Christian counseling is not to be done in a corner. Christian counselors do not belong to some secret society that refuses to allow its practitioners to divulge secrets.

In Paul's comments about eternity, Paul also speaks of time (the right season). When God works in time He works according to a schedule that He, Himself, has devised. How creatures, created in His image, think they

Titus 1

4 to Titus, who is a true child according to the faith that we share: help and peace from God the Father and from Christ Jesus our Savior.

---

can get along without plans and schedules, which they (like God) must follow, doing things "just at the right time," is beyond me. If God plans His work and then works His plan, so must your counselees. There are counselees whose problems are wholly the result of poor planning (or the simple lack of it), and there are some who while planning fairly well, never implement or follow through those plans.

Even when planning is not the principal problem, it can become a complicating problem, hindering genuine change in other areas. All change requires planning, scheduling, implementing and follow through. Often then, you will fail to help if you do not recognize a counselee's potential difficulty in this area and take steps to avoid it. What should you do? Well, there are many things you can do, specifically, but they all boil down to one essential: you must "ride herd" on the counselee. That means, you much check—every week—to be sure that commitments are being kept. And, you must deal with all impediments to keeping those commitments. Part of the discipline needed to bring about change has to do with making and keeping schedules. As God keeps His promises, so should His children keep theirs. Of course, if *you* are undisciplined, unstructured, and fail to plan and schedule, you will not be able to help others. One essential for good counseling is structured living on the part of the one doing counseling.

Having completed the introductory words found in verses 1 through 3, Paul now addresses the epistle to "Titus," whom he calls "a true child according to the faith that we share." He wants the Cretans to know that they can trust Titus implicitly. Titus' faith is correct; they can count on his teaching to be the same as Paul's. He will not lead them astray. And, for Titus, he wishes "grace" (here, the word means "help") and "peace." Like every counselor, he will need both in the work Paul has sent him to do. The very same help and peace is available to all of God's true children. Counselees (and even counselors, at times) may not think so, but if they have not received it, you can be sure that there is something wrong. Perhaps (1) your counselee is not a true child of God. Possibly, (2) if a true child, he has been very disobedient to his Father Who is waiting for repentance from him before granting help and peace. Or, (3) both help and peace are on the way but...God's timetable may not correspond to the counselee's. And, (4) in some cases, the counselee may have gone about

Christian Counselor's Commentary

> **5** The reason why I left you behind in Crete was so that you might set straight those things that were left undone, and appoint elders in every city according to the program that I laid out for you—

---

trying to obtain help and peace in unbiblical ways. Counselors, in those cases, must turn the counselee around toward God's ways. Then, too, (5) both help and peace (particularly the latter) are ordinarily by-products, not to be sought in and of themselves, but to be received as the result of obedience to commands (this point will be developed in greater detail when considering Philippians 4). You may wish to pursue these various options with those who claim to seek help and peace but have failed to obtain either. At any rate, it will be well to keep them in mind.

Having written these important introductory words, Paul now launches into the letter itself. He begins by reminding Titus (and any Cretans who might have questioned his commission) of the reason he was left behind. Paul had left many things "undone." He was not happy about that; something had to be done to tie up loose ends. Titus would set things straight. It was not like Paul to leave before completing his work. Because of some necessity, he had been called away before doing so. What happened, we do not know. But, we do know that he was unhappy about the disorganized conditions he left. To tidy things up, he left his trusted companion and co-worker Titus behind. Counselors too must concern themselves with completing the work that they begin. It is possible, however, that like Paul, there may be times when they cannot. It is important, then, to lean on trusted companions to whom you can turn when needed. If there is no one like that at present, it would be wise to begin training someone right away. Like Paul, you need a team. Could you begin with an elder or deacon, perhaps? Take him into several counseling cases with you. Let him see how it is done. Discuss these cases together. Teach him some basic principles; lend him some of the principal books about nouthetic counseling that are available. Get him ready, and when he is, actually entrust some counseling situations to him. But, always be ready to back him up if he gets stuck or needs your authority. (As we have seen, one purpose of this letter is just that.) Training others is essential to good counseling. We often speak of all that **Paul** accomplished (and, of course, he did accomplish much). But sometimes we forget that Paul was the leader of a **team**. He had organized and trained a number of men to whom he could entrust matters such as this when necessity arose. If you are trying to "go it alone," counselor, you are making a large mistake. Even Moses couldn't do that.

6 whoever is beyond suspicion, is the husband of only one wife, who has trustworthy children not open to a charge of incorrigibility or rebellion.
7 An overseer, as God's steward, must be beyond suspicion, not one who wants his own way, not hot-headed, not dependent on wine, not a fighter, nor greedy for money;

Paul was concerned about bringing **order** out of the unsettled and disorderly conditions he left behind, something he would have seen to personally if it had been possible. Therefore, Titus was to follow **the program** that Paul had **laid out for him**. The word here is used of provisions set forth in a will. Paul's wishes, laid out beforehand, were to be followed to the letter. He did not merely set Titus out on his own. Paul had developed goals and methodology for founding and organizing congregations that he followed everywhere he went, and it was those that he wanted Titus to follow also. He had gone over it with him before he departed and now, writing at the first opportunity, urges him to get on with the program he had outlined. It began with "appointing" men called "elders" to the task of ruling and teaching the little flocks of believers in each city. Order is important to Christ. His church must do things "decently and in order." The eldership, an office that goes back into the beginnings of Old Testament times and continues in an unbroken succession right up into the New, would become the basis for such order. I shall say more about elders subsequently, but for now, consider for a moment the importance of order *through officers* in the Church. Too many counselors, themselves, are disorderly in the sense that their work is not carried on under the auspices of the elders of Christ's church. No one should free-lance Christian counseling. While all Christians are called upon to counsel informally, those who do so as part of a life calling, formally, should operate within the structure of the Church set forth in the Bible. They should be subject to their brethren in all they do, and be authorized by the church to do it. They themselves should be elders, who bring order to the church in all their work, rather than working outside (often in competition with) it, as some do.

Now, Paul turns to the qualifications for an **elder** whom, in verse 7, he also calls **an overseer** (bishop). Notice how he uses the words interchangeably here and in Acts 20:17, 28. Why does the same man bear a double title? The word "elder" refers to his qualifications—he is to be "mature" in the faith. The word "overseer" speaks of his office, or work. He is a mature Christian man who oversees that flock of God in a particular location.

Christian Counselor's Commentary

> 8 rather, he must be hospitable, one who loves whatever is good, self-restrained, fair, holy, self-controlled,

But back to the elder qualifications that Paul laid down. The first speaks of his reputation: **he is beyond suspicion** (i.e., no charge can be leveled against him). He has **only one wife** (i.e., he is not polygamous. Polygamy was common among Jews, who were numerous in Crete.) He has children in his home **who are loyal** to their parents and not open to charges of **unsalvageableness** or **rebellion** (The word is used of untamed animals and means "wild").[1] The shepherdly overseer, who is also a steward of the things of God, Paul repeats, must be **beyond suspicion** (in motives, in dispensing truth, handling of money, etc.). He must not always **insist on his own way, nor be hotheaded** (one who loses control). He must not be **addicted to wine**, not be **a fist-fighter**, nor be **greedy for money**. Those qualities are, of course, minimal. Some want to raise the qualifications so high that no one would fit. But, not a fist-fighter? Has only one wife? These, surely, are minimal. Moreover, positively, he must be **hospitable**, one who **loves whatever is good, sensible** (or, self-restrained), **fair, holy, self-controlled** (lit., "having a grip on one's self"). And, doctrinally, he must **hold firmly to** (the word indicates, "against pressure to let go of") the **teachings of the Scriptures,** which, of course, are dependable.

Now, there is a lot of material. What should we do with it? To begin with, you should recognize that this list of qualifications pertains not only to elders, but to every counselor. Is there one item on the list with which you could dispense and still call a counselor acceptable? Certainly not.[2] Then, let us look at the qualifications in that light.

The counselor should not be suspect. How can you accept advice from a person whose motives are questionable? One against whom charges of an offense are plausible? If he has acted or spoken in ways that throw doubt on his integrity as a person, or as leader in the Church, he has severely weakened his ability to counsel. If people doubt his morality, he cannot be held up as a counselor. His reputation must be unsullied. If he were polygamous (a problem still encountered on mission fields), he would lose status as an example for the flock, since in Christ's church the

---

1. Cf. Eli's sons: I Sam. 2:22-25; 3:13.
2. This certainly reinforces the fact that those who counsel as a life calling should be qualified for the work by ordination as elders.

Titus 1

9 holding firmly to the teaching of the trustworthy Word, that he may be able both to encourage by healthy teaching, and convict of their error those who object.

---

ideal is monogamy. Uncontrolled children indicate that there is something wrong with the training and management of his own family. Thus, he will be unable to help others in their family difficulties. He must be a reliable person, someone you can depend upon. And, he must not stubbornly insist on what he wants. People like that not only are difficult to get along with, they can be very frustrating in any type of cooperative venture, such as solving counseling problems. Hotheaded persons lack patience—a cardinal virtue of good counselors. There are setbacks, disappointments and the like in all counseling. One cannot lose his composure when things don't go right. He must not be addicted. How can he help addicts when he, himself, has been unable to overcome addiction? And, if you put a physically-oriented person in the counseling room, you are asking for serious trouble. Probably, within six months he will be arrested for assault. Because people who are in trouble are extremely vulnerable, and they must rely upon the advice of another, they are subject to every sort of scam. A counselor, greedy for money, will soon become slick enough to figure out innumerable ways of helping people part with their funds. A hospitable counselor, on the other hand, will go out of his way to accommodate persons truly in need. As a lover of what is good, he will always be thinking of what is best for his counselee. He will need to be self-restrained when a counselee spits out angry words or makes ridiculous accusations against him, as so often they unfairly do. And, in dealing with matters of church discipline or arbitration, he must be rigidly fair. He may not be a respecter of persons. His life must be set apart to God in such a way that others know they are inquiring of a man of God. There must be a basic, unalloyed purity of life and motive. Those are the personal attributes that he must acquire in order to counsel well.

If you agree that these are the basic qualifications for a Christian counselor, then you also ought to agree that counseling cannot rightly be carried on by anyone who is not a Christian. Obviously, no unbeliever can pass the qualifications listed by Paul. Not all Christians can. It is the obligation of biblical counselors and all those in authority in the Church to make this fact known to members who may be inclined to send loved ones to non-christian counselors. Unbelievers, for instance, do not "hold fast" to God's reliable Word (v. 9). How, then, can they direct counselees into "the paths of righteousness?"

In addition to previous qualifications which largely have to do with one's spiritual life, the biblical counselor must understand the teachings of Scripture, systematically and accurately, and hold firmly to them (without doubting or compromising under pressure) so that **he may be able both to encourage by healthy teaching, and convict of their error those who object** (v. 9). To realize these two objectives one must acquire a thorough knowledge of the Scriptures. Each objective needs to be unpacked.

First, look at the importance of encouragement. Paul says that encouragement comes from healthy teaching. We see how it did when Paul straightened out the understanding of the Thessalonians (I Thess. 4:13ff.) by teaching the truth about the Lord's coming and the resurrection, and then said, "Encourage one another with these words" (4:18). Clearly, it was Paul's "healthy words" spoken to grieving Christians that made it possible to encourage them.

The word translated **to encourage** (*parakaleo*) is a large one. Its fundamental meaning is "to assist." Some have thought that it ought to be the term for counseling, but it is not specific enough. At times it *may* mean "give assistance by counseling," but, at other times it may mean "assist by urging, persuading, comforting," or, as here, by *encouraging*. Many of your counselees need divine encouragement. That encouragement will not be found in the assurances of men or by locking on to one's own supposed inner resources. Visualization techniques and healing of the memories do not have any scriptural basis and, therefore, are inadequate, and, even harmful because, by pointing counselees to a wrong answer, they also point them away from the true one. It is in the Word, the Scriptures of the Old and New Testaments, that encouragement will be found. Paul reiterates this fact in Romans 15:4. In the Scriptures there is truth (John 17:17), and it is the "healthy" words of truth, alone, that bring true peace and joy. These words the biblical counselor ministers to those who come for help. He teaches not only the commandments of God that bring life and peace, and shows counselees how to live by them, but he also teaches him the promises of God on which he may rely. It is that, in particular, that the apostle has in view in this place: he emphasizes that the Word, in which these promises are found, is **trustworthy, reliable** (v. 9). You, too, may bring hope to defeated, downcast counselees by unfolding, explaining and applying the never-failing promises of the Bible. No book in all the world

Titus 1

10 There are many rebellious persons, vain-talkers, and deceivers, especially of the circumcision party,

---

has as much hope packed into its pages as the Bible; and its promises are all as certain as the One Who gave them!

The, counselor must know the Scriptures in order to **convict of their error those who object.** There will be counselees—and, often, more to the point, those influencing them—who will object to your teaching. You must be ready to refute their objections by biblical wisdom. Sometimes, people piously say, "The Bible needs no defense; just teach it and let the chips fall where they may." Well, of course the Bible needs no defense, but your teaching from the Bible does! There are those who oppose the pure teaching of Scripture, and they must be brought to conviction of their sin in doing so. The word "convict" is a legal term that means "to so prosecute the case against someone that he is *convicted* (pronounced guilty) of the crime of which he is accused." God expects you to press the truth of Scripture so strongly against those who oppose it that they are convicted of their "error." You must know the answers not only to the objections to Scripture, but also the answers to the answers to your answers!"

You say, "According to the verse I just quoted, Phil, it is clear that God expects you to change." Phil replies, "I'm too old to change. You can't teach an old dog new tricks." You must be able to answer that objection. You might respond, "I don't know—I'm not an animal trainer. But I know one thing: you're not an old dog. You are a human being created in the image of God and redeemed by His Son. And, by God's grace, you will change. Let me tell you what happened to Abraham when he was 99 years old..." You must learn to use Scripture to convict those who oppose. It is important to list those objections that people raise, to which you do not have an immediate biblically-derived response. Then pray about and study them until you have answers ready for the next objector. So, as in all the ministry of the elders, counselors must be prepared to use the Bible for the two purposes listed in verse 9.

Paul continues to discuss those people who object, focusing in the next seven verses on those who both within and without the Church need to be refuted and their errors exposed. No counselor who believes that error harms and truth helps can afford to ignore the important ministry of **convicting of error** about which Paul writes. Those in error are not few in number: **there are many rebellious persons, vain-talkers, and deceivers, especially of the circumcision party**, says the apostle. Over the cen-

Christian Counselor's Commentary

turies, the numbers have only increased. And the parties. But the heresies and the attitudes have not varied much. There are still those who, like the circumcision party, wish to impose requirements in addition to repentance and faith for salvation. All such efforts on the part of the potential counselee or those influencing him must be countered. That is part of the task of the elder-counselor. Opposition to any effort to add to or remove anything from the simple good news of Christ's death and resurrection is essential. Such teaching must be suppressed. Moreover, all those teachings that amount to legalistic additions to the Bible must be dealt with as well; don't allow anyone to place the word of man on the same level as the Word of God. To do so is the essence of legalism.

Notice what kinds of people false teachers are and the sorts of things they do. They are, Paul tells us, "rebellious, vain-talkers and deceivers." That is an interesting combination of characteristics. Ever meet counselees with such personality problems? You can be sure that they will cause trouble in Christ's church. Rebellion is like the sin of witchcraft, Samuel told Saul; it is serious business, not to be taken lightly. These people rebel against God by rebelling against His teachers and the truth they proclaim. You remember Korah who, together with Dathan and Abiram rebelled against Moses and Aaron, wanting to assume their authority. God was so displeased He was ready to wipe out the entire people. Moses interceded, and the ground opened and the rebels and all who stood with them were swallowed up. That is what God thinks of rebellion. You must faithfully convey His sentiments wherever necessary. There are those who at a wink would rebel against the leadership of a church to which they belong, violating rightful authority, if they thought they could get a following—or, perhaps, even your support. Look out for those who speak subversively in counseling. Don't for a moment entertain or encourage their talk; rebuke them for it and warn them of the dire consequences that might come from it. Every counselor must stand firmly against the rebellious spirit of any who come for counseling.

The people mentioned here are "vain-talkers." They are full of hot air. They talk about what they believe and how they intend to change, but it is all talk. Such people are easily detected in counseling. They never follow through. They will not do their "homework" (assignments given for the coming week[1]). When they fail, and you attempt to discover what went wrong in order to help them rectify it, you meet nothing but hesi-

---

1. See copious material concerning "Homework" in *The Christian Counselor's Manual* (Zondervan, 1973).

Titus 1

11 whose mouths must be shut because they are upsetting whole households by teaching things that they shouldn't for the sake of shameful gain.

---

tancy, complaining and/or lame excuses. This sorry attitude cannot be tolerated in counseling. People must mean business with God. If they do not, and, after extensive help, will not change their attitudes, there is little to do but cease counseling and institute church discipline. If you cannot effect change, don't go on encouraging idleness and indifference by coddling such counselees. Paul's words are clear—**their mouths must be shut!** (v. 11)

And, again, you will counsel **deceivers**. Deception, often, is more difficult to discern than vain talk and rebellion (especially, the latter). By its very nature, it uses stealth to cover up its motives and objectives. Proficient deceivers are among those who are most trying. Like vain-talkers they will promise anything, but they will lie about why they failed to perform. Yet, the same factor that exposes empty talk also uncovers deception: homework. When you build each week's assignment on the claims of what has been done during the previous week and the commitments made in the counseling session, if these are lies, you will soon (usually, in a week or two) recognize the fact. Homework based on lies never works out. And when you thoroughly examine why it failed, at length you will uncover the deception. Deception may, of course, not only be directed toward you. The counselee may be involved in deceiving a spouse, the church or others. Not for a moment can it be tolerated. Deceivers must be convicted of their sin and brought to repentance. Then, they must be taught how to substitute truth-telling for deception (Cf. Eph. 4:25).

Don't be surprised if occasionally you find all three traits lumped together in the same person, as Paul seems to indicate was true of these false teachers. When that occurs, at once it makes your task more difficult—and easier. More difficult, naturally, because you have more to do. Easier, in that you are more likely to notice that there is something wrong earlier in the game; you will have three indications of that fact. Actually, it is highly probable that where one tendency is present, the other two are present as well, with only one, or possibly two, predominating. The thing to do then is, where you find one, look hard to see if, to a smaller extent, you do not also find the others.

In verse 11, Paul says that these deceivers must be countered by elders so as to shut their mouths (the image in the word "shut" is putting a plug in the top of a pipe or jar). That is strong language, not precisely

> 12 One of themselves—one of their own prophets—said, "Cretans are always liars, evil beasts, lazy gluttons."

what modern, weak Christians frequently advocate. Paul was not weak. While he practiced meekness, that did not mean weakness. There is a time to exercise every one of the emotions. When the flock is in danger, the true shepherd takes up his "rod" (a kind of cudgel mentioned in Psalm 23) to drive off the wild beast. That too is a part of good counsel. Whole households were at stake. False doctrine was being spewed out, Paul says, *in order to realize "shameful gain."* Cretan love of money was well-known; Livy, Plutarch and Polybius all commented on it. The problem did not vanish with the first century church. As we all know from national exposes, it is very much a part of the religious culture of our day. That means that when the counselor recognizes that his counselee is about to be "taken," he will deal with the fact. Lives are ruined by religious shysters concerned about little else than making money. When it appears that your counselee has fallen prey to one of these you must confront him about the fact, not shy away as many do. But—and this is important—get the facts before making accusations (cf. II Corinthians 13:1). Not only will you be unable to convince the counselee apart from hard data, but you may find yourself involved in slander, or a lawsuit.

Now, as verse 12 seems to indicate, these troublemakers in the church were from Crete itself. There were, of course, many Jewish settlements all around the Mediterranean. Their congregations became the first preaching points for Paul and his team as they moved into new communities. It is possible that some of them, as in other places (such as Thessalonica) formed opposition groups to the apostles' efforts (in v. 10 he does specifically mention the "circumcision party"). But, if they were the nucleus of the opposition, they were long-standing Cretans, who, for generations had lived there and had adopted many of the characteristics of the native population. We know this because of the words of verse 12. The quotation accusing the Cretans of being **always liars, evil beasts, lazy gluttons** is from Epimenides (also repeated by Callimachus). Epimenides was highly regarded. Plato called him a "divine man" and the Cretans offered sacrifices to him. Livy and other writers of the ancient world also have little good to say of the Cretans. Paul claims that the words of the poet were true (v. 13). So, he is careful to warn his readers that these national characteristics would adversely affect the church if people exhibiting them were allowed to persist unchanged within its membership. It is,

Titus 1

13 This testimony is true. For this reason, rebuke them sharply, that their faith may remain healthy,

---

he maintains, the task of the elders to **sharply rebuke** any members who tended to exhibit these traits. Lying and deceit destroy congregations. Acting like animals (**beasts**), rather than like redeemed human beings, is characteristic of the violence and self-centered gratification also widely seen in our time in this country. Christians must distantiate themselves from the culture at this point. Counselors will find themselves giving counter-cultural advice no matter the country in which they live. And laziness and gluttony fit the national picture of Cretans as well.

Whenever elders find these characteristics taking hold of members of the church, they are to "rebuke them sharply." This last word, "sharply," must not be watered down. That is precisely what Paul wrote. The word is used of the surgeon's knife. I suppose we should take it from him that certain combinations of characteristics, comprising a lifestyle, will respond to nothing less than sharp (stinging, cutting) rebukes. A sharp rebuke, like the sharp point of a goad, is *felt*. That is the point that Paul makes. How does that sound to you, counselor? Do you see yourself sharply rebuking anyone in counseling? Have you been trained in a form of counseling that employs and reaches only some, but not all, of the human emotions? Well, if so, there is an important instrument missing from your black, leather bag. It is not pleasant to rebuke sharply. Yet, that is precisely what Paul orders. If you think that the apostle was wrong in his approach, then you are doubting the inspiration of the Holy Spirit. It was not merely Paul who advocated this method of dealing with such persons, it was the Spirit of God in him driving him to write as he did. You have a bigger problem to handle than the problem of a sharp rebuke; your problem has to do with the matter of inspiration itself.

If you don't doubt that the Spirit "moved" Paul to write these words, but admit that the problem is in yourself ("I don't know if I could ever bring myself to rebuke anyone sharply"), you must work on it. First, recognize that just as Paul expected them to change at his rebuke, through repentance, so too, he expects you to make the changes requisite for becoming a counselor who is fully-armed with every weapon in the Word. Your personality is a combination of the genetic makeup you had nothing to do with and how you have habituated it to respond to life situations. It is because personality is not wholly (or even mainly) genetic, but learned, that you can change. By doing what God commands in the Scriptures,

Christian Counselor's Commentary

14 not paying attention to Jewish myths and commandments of people who turn away from the truth.

---

whether you feel like it or not, in time you will change. Very shy persons, obeying the Bible have turned into bold defenders of the flock. Look how Peter changed. You can too. Stop telling yourself you can't. If you do not believe God can change you, counselor, how can you effectively counsel others to change?

One thing to keep in mind, that should help, is the reason for the sharp rebuke. The rebuke is designed to keep the faith of the sheep **healthy**. Lazy, gluttonous Christians, who lie and act according to their physical desires (as animals do), are not healthy. The sharp rebuke, like the sharp knife of the surgeon, is wielded, not to injure, but to heal. But, of course, it does hurt. There is pain. Yet in a world of sin suffering is inevitable. Until you are willing to pick up the verbal knife and do surgery, you are not fit for counseling. Love for your counselees is what drives counselors who care to hurt in order to heal.

It seems as if the large Jewish population on Crete was what Paul had in mind (cf. Josephus, *Ant.*, 17:12:1). He returns to the Jewish problem, now speaking of **Jewish myths** and the false **commandments of men** (v. 14), and with one stroke of his brush, does away with both. Christians are to "pay no attention" to such things. What were these myths? Doubtless some of the oral traditions and those found in the apocrypha and pseudepigrapha. What were the commandments of men? Certainly, that body of man-made rules to which Jesus referred when he taught that these made the Word of God of non-effect (cf. also Mt. 15:9). Both silly speculation and legalistic laws invented by the Pharisees must be ignored. That is important for you to understand. People today will come for counseling who are confused about matters that create problems for them *unnecessarily*. Don't bother to argue about such issues; instead, avoid them and turn your counselees back to the Scriptures. Let them know that the Bible alone is the foundation for living, and therefore, for your counseling. Refuse to get bogged down debating extra-biblical speculation or legalistic views in which your counselee may become entangled. Simply observe that these matters are not biblical issues, but arise out of human thinking, and that you do not wish to waste time debating them. If you can steer counselees away from such things, while helping them through imparting the life-giving words of the Bible, at the end you can point out that the matters you brushed aside (as Paul did) are not really all that

Titus 1

15 Everything is clean to those who themselves are clean; but to those who are dirty and unbelieving nothing is clean, but both their minds and consciences are dirty.

---

important after all. Counselees, helped by following Scripture, will be in a much better position to reject these issues altogether when at length, after help, they are able to get some perspective on them. These foolish Jewish teachings didn't help at all; they only confused. The Word of God did. You may make the contrast, then urge counselees to pay no more attention to them.

The point that Paul is making is that when people turn to myths and human commandments, they turn away from the Word ("truth"). God's Word is truth (John 17:17); it alone sanctifies. Human commandments and myths do not. That, then, is the approach Paul would have you take.

In verse 15, Paul continues to refer to Jewish problems; here, ceremonies. He agrees with Jesus that all meats, etc., have now been cleansed (see also Acts 10:15; I Tim. 4:4, 5). The Jewish clean/unclean ritual and ceremonial laws were put aside by the coming of Jesus Christ. Cleanliness, today, of which Old Testament laws were but the type, is a matter of one's inner attitude. The issues are discussed in I Corinthians and in Romans 14, when dealing with meats offered to idols. That is clean about which one has no doubts. If someone eats, thinking that eating may be a sin (even when the act itself is not), he sins because he went ahead and did something that he thought might be a violation of God's law ("whatever is not of faith is sin"—Rom. 14:23). His attitude (not his act) was sinful. And he should repent. There is no such thing as "false guilt." There may be a faulty basis for the guilt, but the guilt is real.

But, Paul is saying more than that in this place. He observes that dirty minds make everything else dirty. Nothing is clean to the one whose mind dirties it. Looking through a dirty automobile windshield, everything,—even that which is clean—looks dirty. Unbelief, as he notes, goes along with filthy thinking. We have seen that in a thousand ways in our society. When a mind is dirty, one puts the wrong spin on everything. He may make sexual innuendoes about the most innocent matter. He may see bad motives in others when there are none. He may bend the truth to fit his viewpoint. Watch out for this dynamic in your counselees. When you notice how everything and everybody else is wrong (according to your counselee), you may suspect that he is a person with a defiled mind. Everything entering it becomes defiled by the dirt that is packed tightly

Christian Counselor's Commentary

16 They claim to know God but they deny Him by what they do. They are abominable and disobedient and have failed in doing every good work.

---

therein. Defiled consciences are consciences that no longer work right. They fail to make the proper assessments of thoughts and acts, and as a result, fail to alert one to his sin. A person like this is in real trouble. He must repent of much. You must help him see from God's Word how dirty his thinking is. You must become his conscience for a while (using the Scripture as your standard, of course). He doesn't know how to determine right from wrong: you must evangelize and then teach him.

Finally, verse 16 concludes this section. Here are people who profess faith in Christ, but their faith is not genuine. They claim to know God, but deny Him by their works. Words and works; faith and faithfulness—it's the same old question again. If, after enough proper biblical help one fails to show any progress, you may readily suspect that the failure of good, and the prevalence of bad works is indicative of false faith. Of course, your suspicion may be confirmed only when church discipline, properly exercised, has failed and the person is removed from the church. You have no right as an individual to make that determination about a so-called Christian. That is a matter for the church, *as such*, to decide. When the church does, he is then to be treated as a "heathen" and a "publican" (both of whom were outside the church). Such people are not really counselees. They ought to be evangelized. Paul calls them abominable and disobedient. How could they be less when they fail **in doing every good work?** In this letter Paul, like every effective counselor, is deeply concerned about his counselees doing good deeds. Every chapter, as I have noted earlier, concludes with some comment about good deeds (cf. 2:14; 3:14).

While no one is saved by good works, his profession of faith and salvation is evaluated as true or false by their presence or absence: "By their fruits you will know them (Matthew 7:20)." And, that fact ought to be clear to every counselor. Unbelievers are disobedient, do abominable things and fail in their attempts to do good at every turn. That is not something that should surprise you. It didn't surprise Paul. He was concerned, nevertheless, about Christians who were affected by such people. And he wanted to guard the flock from them. Counselors, who of necessity touch the nerve of the persons in a congregation at the very points that have been just mentioned in these verses, must be concerned too.

Chapter 2

1 But as for you, speak things that are in keeping with healthy teaching.

Verse 1 is transitional. Paul has excoriated the false teachers who are upsetting the flock, warned Titus and his people to stay away from them, urged elders to rebuke those who are being influenced by them and insisted that the church pay no attention to empty speculation and life-restricting rules. Now, in contrast, Paul tells Titus, unlike the false teachers, "You" must "speak the things that are in keeping with healthy teaching." What one preaches and says in counseling, as he ministers the Word, brings spiritual life and health to those who listen with faith. If the little churches, in many of Crete's hundred cities, were already sickly because of infection from false doctrine, that which would heal them is the Scriptures—health-giving true doctrine of the Word of God. That is something for every counselor to remember: he does not heal sin-sick souls. It is Bible medicine that he prescribes that does. It is crucial, then, for every counselor both to know the Scriptures—which passages apply to which problems—and to know how to administer them to those in trouble. "Healthy teaching" (called "sound teaching" in the KJV) is teaching that promotes spiritual health. It consists of Scripture ministered as the counselor's advice. Words spoken in counseling, just as in preaching, help or hurt, heal or injure. Your words can never be neutral. When they are thoroughly biblical in content and manner, they will be health-giving.

Some of those healthy words that every man of God must "speak" are found in the two chapters that remain. These chapters are a goldmine of truth. The wise counselor will find himself digging away in them constantly. He will discover information that will not only help him to firm up his own thinking, but the material he unearths he can convey with salutary effect to counselees of all sorts. Learn all you can about these two chapters and they will keep your thinking and your counseling on track.

Paul categorizes distinct groups, in general, as needing particular kinds of help. He begins with the older, presumably more mature, members of the congregations. Older men, he says, must be taught. Some older men will not allow others—especially if they are younger—to teach them anything. They think age alone is sufficient to carry them through. Few things are more tragic than to see an older man or woman still tenaciously

Christian Counselor's Commentary

2   Older men must be taught to be levelheaded, serious, self-restrained, healthy in faith, in love, and in endurance.

---

holding to opinions, most of which have been proven faulty over and over through the years. Titus is not to let age become a barrier; he must teach older members of the congregations as well as the younger.

But what must older men be taught? Six things are listed as peculiarly important for the more mature. **Levelheadedness** comes first. How many counselees begin life unstable, wild and careless, and continue to act according to these early-developed patterns throughout their years! Well, the Christian counselor must wade in and do something about those patterns. He must shatter those that hinder levelheaded thinking and action while replacing them with those that promote it. What is levelheaded thinking and acting? It refers to well-measured, careful thinking and action that accords with reality as it is in God's world. This reality, naturally, is not what unbelievers suppose reality to be. Instead, it is reality as it truly is—as it accords with God's way of looking at things. A levelheaded or sober person is one who is not intoxicated with the world's stupefying wine. It is one who has been sobered up by the coming of the Holy Spirit into his life so that he is able to understand and do those things that please god. This is precisely what many older counselees need to "be taught." You can be sure of that because Paul not only includes it in his list, but thinks of it *first*. In a sense, levelheadedness is the overall result of the remaining five. When they are in place, a person may be said to be levelheaded. A levelheaded person never goes overboard. He speaks and acts in ways that commend him to others. He is balanced and, while cautious and careful in making decisions, nevertheless, having made them, acts. Levelheaded persons know how to evaluate accurately and what to do in most situations. When they do not, they do not become flustered, angry or frustrated; they find out. Levelheadedness is lacking in many counselees.

To be **serious** is the next item on Paul's list. The word has deteriorated—like so many words in our language. Here it means dignified, but not gloomy or dour. It is the dignity of one who knows what he is doing, one with sound judgment. To be serious is to understand what circumstances must not be treated lightly. It is the ability to weigh and sift and act accordingly. It is the quality that is possessed by a person who faces up to grave situations with the solemnity they require, the ability to treat weighty and profound issues for what they are. A serious person knows when to turn off levity and get down to business. Older Christian men

Titus 2

should be examples of seriousness, since much of life—and death—is serious business.

Next on Paul's list is **self-restraint.** Self-restraint is the capacity for self-control given as a part of the fruit of the Spirit. In addition, it includes sensible thinking that leads to handling one's self well in difficult situations. How older counselees, who have allowed themselves free reign throughout the years, need to learn structure and discipline that is provided by God's Word through His Spirit! How undignified it is to see an older man grow red around the neck and eventually blow up. There is a calming influence of the truth that allows one to put up with every sort of offense knowing that one is right with God.

Healthy (sound) in faith. That is item number four. Again, many older men (I think men, in particular) think that it is too late to begin learning the ins-and-outs of the faith. They are so wrong. Probably, for the first time—you may need to point out—they will have enough time on their hands to do some significant study of truth. Since age has required them to slow down in the doing of other things (perhaps they have been retired), one of the few things they can take up with new vigor is a study of the Scriptures. Certainly, the lazy, worthless pursuit of TV cannot be condoned! One is healthy in faith when he knows what the Lord teaches in His Word and has learned to put it into practice in his life.

Healthy (sound) in love. That is item number five. When his life is strong in the showing of love to God and to others, it is a spiritually healthy one. But not until. Let older persons read the Gospel of John and the Book of I John if they want to undertake a study of what the Bible means by love and how one shows it in life. Nothing could be a greater testimony to the world than a loving older man who lives according to biblical injunctions. It is that sort of life Paul commends to the older men.

Finally, he enjoins **endurance.** That is the ability to hang in there when the going gets tough. Tough things happen when one begins to age. Loss is one of those. The loss of friends, health, hearing sight, property, work—you name it. But those who love the Lord and seek to serve Him, increasingly find that He fills the empty spots. That is what you, as a counselor, must help older men to believe and experience.

Teaching is an important part of counseling. Contrary to many other methods of counseling, Christian counseling always involves teaching from the Word of God. So, it is understandable that in spite of the failure of many religions in Christ's day to teach women, and the reluctance of the Jews to do so, Christianity is strong on the point: **Older women, similarly, must be taught...**The word "likewise" or **similarly** shows that

Christian Counselor's Commentary

> **3** Older women, similarly, must be taught to conduct themselves with an outward bearing that is appropriate to holy persons, not being slanderers, nor slaves of much wine. They must be teachers of what is good

there is to be no distinction in the education of women or men in the Christian church. Both, "similarly," are to be taught. That it is the *fact* of teaching that is "similar," rather than its content, is clear from the fact that *what is taught* older men and women is appropriate to each and, therefore, differs in content, and the only similarity is in the fact of teaching itself. Paul wants it to be known that it is just as important to teach women as it is to teach men.

What must the older women be taught? First, **to conduct themselves with an outward bearing that is appropriate to holy persons**. To what does Paul refer? Let us understand the terms used. The two words "holy persons" in the original is one term, which, literally, means "priestess-like." Obviously, there are no priests or priestesses in the Christian religion, so, what does this mean? It means that she is to live as one who, in all matters of life, lives dedicated to the service of God. One like that is going to impress others with her demeanor and general deportment. That is the idea behind the words translated **conduct themselves with an outward bearing...** This term often has to do with outward "dress" (Cf. I Tim. 2:9), but here speaks of inner qualities that show up in one's outer carriage. What Paul is saying is that you ought to **know** this woman is dedicated to the service of the Lord by the way in which she carries on day by day in observable ways. That is a very laudable goal to set before older women in counseling. And it is one that a serious-minded believing woman should be glad to accept from a younger man.

They are also to avoid gossip and **slander**. Nothing characterizes the devil more than "slander." The word devil means "slanderer." This sentence reads in the Greek "not being *devils.*" Perhaps because their greater interest in people, women, rather than men (whose interest is often more in things) tend to gossip and slander others. At any rate, women are here warned against the tendency. Much counseling is occasioned by loose talk. No wonder Paul deals with the problem. You must not be hesitant to do so either. Indeed, it is also a problem of the counselor—man or woman—since he too is interested in people and their affairs. It is of the greatest importance that he neither encourage counselees nor allow them to talk negatively about those who are not present. That certainly is forbidden by the many passages in Proverbs and elsewhere that condemn

Titus 2

4 so that they may train the young women to show affection to their husbands and to their children,

---

gossip, and may readily turn into slander. Because the counselee is all-too-ready to speak negatively, and because the counselor is interested in gathering information, the very structure of the situation creates a strong temptation to violate biblical teaching at this point. Do not succumb! And, when you are counseling women—particularly older ones—always remain alert to what they are saying about others. It is so easy to slip into slander and gossip when gathering information.

One way to avoid the problem is to set up correct expectations from the beginning. When the other person is not present, you might want to say something like this: "Now, since so-and-so is not here, we are going to have to be extremely careful not to cross the line from gathering information about the structure of the problem into gossip and slander about the person. I will listen carefully and let you know whenever we might seem to be approaching forbidden territory." Along with those comments, you might also want to quote one or more of the verses (including this one) that forbid such talk.

And older women must not become **slaves to much wine**. Few things can destroy an older woman's Christian testimony sooner than addiction. Instead, she, herself, must become **a teacher of what is good**. It is plain that addiction and teaching younger women do not go together since biblical teaching, as we have seen, involves modeling (cf. comments on I Thessalonians 1). Older women, then, must become examples to the younger. The teaching that is under consideration is **training**, or as that word means, "schooling that makes one sane or sensible." They are to work with the younger women in practical ways.

Now, in our era when feminism pervades the church, it is time for Christian women to learn what it is that **God** has ordained for them. Counselors, faced with women who are complaining that they are not allowed to teach, should point out to them that they not only may teach, but that they **must**. God commands women mature in the faith to train those who are younger. Since they are to train children as well, that means that two thirds of the teaching task is allocated to them. It is time for them to stop complaining and to get about the task to which God called them. Congregations should provide opportunities for their mature women to exercise their abilities in fulfilling the requirements in these verses.

They should also train women how to do so. The word in the phrase

5 to be self-restrained, pure, housekeepers, kind, submitting themselves to their husbands, that God's Word may not be blasphemed.

---

younger women, might be translated "recently married women." Surely they need the sort of training that is mentioned in verses 4 and 5, but it would also be appropriate in part, at least, to train those who are approaching marriage. Plainly, here is the place where others in the congregation, rather than the pastor or elders, can do a superior job of teaching. And it is their duty to employ them in such activities. Titus' task and yours is to teach the older women how to train the younger ones. Not only are there things on Paul's agenda for training that women know more about than men, but the contact of older women with younger ones is a safer teaching situation. There is less likelihood of temptation from either side. As I have suggested elsewhere, counselors must learn not to take the entire counseling load upon themselves. When it comes to training the younger women in the items listed here they should call on mature women to help.

Well, what does Paul have on his agenda? Seven items, all of which he wants them to practice **that God's Word not be blasphemed** (v. 5^b). The world judges Christianity by its women. There are few things that a counselor does that strengthen the practical apologetic of the church as much as when he helps Christian women live as they ought. Women, acting like the world, while professing to be Christians, probably do as much to downgrade the witness of the church as anything else. So, this is important work—in more ways than one.

One item, in two parts, is the training of younger women **to show affection** (the word is *not* "love" but "affection") **to their husbands and to their children**. We live in a hard, course age, in which mothers abort children, turn on their husbands in violence, and, in general, fail to show that affection that used to be part-and-parcel of femininity. When women began to take over many of the rough-and-ready tasks that traditionally were the province of men, it seems that affection disappeared. Something of that sort must have been true in the Roman world as well. It was a world in which women were much freer to participate in all sorts of activities and tasks than they were allowed to be in the Greek and Hebrew cultures. Perhaps the times were much like they are today. That means that it was important for Paul to encourage training in affection. Older women, who belong to a less violent generation, and who have spent time with the Scriptures that inculcate true femininity, will discover that they have a

Titus 2

mammoth job on their hands. They must buck the present culture (not for the sake of being different, but) in order to raise up a godly generation to succeed them. Many homes would be improved in large measure if there were only some true affection in them. While men must show love, it is principally the women's prerogative to show affection.

Marriage problems are a large part of the counseling enterprise, as you are surely aware. Those who can call upon the help of older women to train younger ones in the fine art of affection (in all that means to husbands and to children), will do a lot for marriages. Much more could be said here about this all-important issue, but I will settle for this: can you right now think of ten ways in which a woman can be affectionate to her husband and ten ways she can show affection to her children? Try writing them down. Did you have trouble? If you are a man, you probably did. If a woman, probably not. Now, men, try this: Ask some mature Christian woman that you think excels in this regard to make the two lists. She can do it in a breeze. Why, then, would you want to go on usurping her place? Why would you go on ignoring Paul's command? If you don't have several older women to whom you can turn for such help, start looking for them and enlisting them—*today*.

The third item is **self-restraint** something we looked at above when Paul was speaking of the older men. Since that is true, we will not repeat what was said there. Item number four is **purity.** It goes without saying that Christian women should keep themselves sexually pure for their future husbands just as those husbands should keep themselves pure for their wives-to-be. With the propaganda abroad today, and the many influences that tend to drive women in another direction, it is imperative that older women spend plenty of time helping younger ones to keep themselves free of these nefarious influences.

Also, the older women must train the younger to become good **housekeepers,** literally, **workers at home.** Many problems stem from failure on the wife's part to keep a good home. All that goes into that ought to be known to older women who have done successfully in this regard, though male counselors could hardly be expected to be so adept. Once more, a recommendation for the older women to take charge.

Kind. That is the next word. Read Ephesians 4: 31, 32 to understand what this word involves. Kindness in the home is one of the finest traits one could cultivate. Counselors must not minimize it. It fits naturally with affection, and is a part of it.

Lastly, but not least, is the wife's **submission** to her husband. **That does not mean becoming a doormat.** It means that she recognizes the

Christian Counselor's Commentary

6 The younger men, similarly, you must encourage to be self-restrained.

---

authority-subjection relationship that God has ordained for this world. Her submission, at bottom, is submission to the Lord. I discuss this subject at length in the appropriate place when considering the Book of Ephesians.

Again, remember it is not the counselor's job to do this training, but to see that the older women do it. That may mean courses taught, encouragement given, instruction on general counseling principles, etc. His task is to orchestrate it; not to do it.

In verse 6, Paul discusses what Titus should teach the young men. They too, like the older men, must learn **self-restraint**. For younger men, often this is much harder. The enthusiasm of youth tends to throw off many restraints. Yet, the counselor has the great privilege of helping younger men mature by emphasizing the importance of this very quality Younger men, learning to restrain both their words and actions, are likely to succeed in life far more often than those who fail to. Moreover, they will find that they are far more able to throw off other irksome and unnecessary restraints when they acquire the ability to restrain themselves. Parents and others are less likely to clap restraints on them when they determine that they, themselves, have developed the capacity for self-restraint. Few things could be more important for counselors to help young people to develop than this capacity for *self*-restraint.

The counselor is to **encourage** young men to learn self-restraint. Encouragement is not the same as demanding. It involves a reasoned approach that is careful at all times not to err in the direction of scolding and censoriousness. It is the approach not of the schoolmarm who demands compliance to her every whim, but rather, the approach of the football coach who, with his arm around the player says, "OK, now let's get in there and do the job—I know you can!" Counselors, particularly when working with youth, need to assume the role of the encourager. When they do, they will discover that they will get much further that they would otherwise. Hear yourself saying to a young man, "All right, John, we know that the Lord wants you to control your temper whenever your father and you disagree. I know it's hard at times. But, it is possible, and by God's grace you can learn to do it. Now this week, go back home and work on it God's way; I know you can. I'll be rooting for you in prayer. And, I'll be waiting to hear great things about it when we get together

Titus 2

> 7 You yourself must exhibit in everything that you do a pattern of fine deeds, integrity in your teaching, seriousness,
> 8 and healthy speech that cannot be censored, so that an opponent may be put to shame because he has nothing bad to say about us.

next week at this time."

And, probably, because he was also a younger man, Titus receives an exhortation from Paul at this place. He is to exhibit in everything a **pattern of good deeds**. That is a stiff assignment. Yet, Paul, himself, was able to point men to the example of his own lifestyle. Every counselor must live in such as way that he, too, is an example in all things to his counselees. That does not mean he will never sin or ever fail his counselee. But, even in these things, he also must set the example. Probably few acts on his part are more important than how he handles his sins and failures—especially in relation to the counselee. If he, who is telling his counselee that he must repent and go to others he has wronged to seek forgiveness, refuses to do so when he wrongs a counselee, he will harm, rather than help. But if he handles his sins well and seeks forgiveness, he will model the thing he wishes to teach in the most powerful way possible.

We have spoken of teaching before. Here the **integrity** of the counselor's teaching is in view. What does that mean? It means that he asserts nothing to be true that he is not sure is taught in the Bible. Integrity also means that when using Scripture, the counselor selects passages that he understands and that he uses them for the purposes for which they were given. Integrity in handling truth is the hallmark of Christian counseling, since it deals in truth from Scripture rather than in the speculations of men. That is true because, as we noted in discussing the first verse of the book, truth is what leads to godliness. To mishandle God's truth in any way means to harm, rather than help, counselees in their Christian growth.

Titus is to be **serious**. Of course! He is dealing with the most serious matter in life: the eternal welfare of his clients. Keeping this before you at all times will have much to do with how you counsel.

And, his **speech** must be **healthy**, speech that **cannot be censored**. That is of the utmost importance to a counselor since, in counseling, he uses *speech* as his primary tool. Speech of the sort here required is speech that, for any reason whatsoever, could be seized on by an **opponent** as inappropriate. It may be misuse of sexual terminology—becoming explicit *in a titillating manner*. Or it may be angry words that break down

Christian Counselor's Commentary

> **9** Slaves must submit to their own masters in everything, seek to satisfy them, but must not talk back to them.

communication. Or it may be the content of words that, when viewed dispassionately, are no better than common gossip about someone who is not present. Or anything else that may be censurable. However, it is important, here, to distinguish those words and statements that violate biblical standards (surely that would be the way of determining) from those that a counselee may **merely claim** to be inappropriate in a Christian counselor. After all, there are times when counselees, in order to justify their sin, become angry with counselors and storm out of the office, claiming all sorts of things that are untrue. Be prepared to be accused of all sorts of things you never did. The counselor must weigh his words carefully, learning to be very *self-critical* so that, so far as he is able to discern, he is sure that he has said nothing to the counselee that enemies of the gospel could use to undermine it. Indeed, wherever it is possible, it is important to have other counselors present, so that your words may be witnessed by that counselor (especially when a man is counseling a woman). All criticism cannot be avoided, of course. Paul and the other disciples—as well as Jesus Himself—were criticized unmercifully. But, here, the point is that the counselor *must do everything he can to avoid giving opponents a handle to grab.*

Note, especially, Paul's use of the word **us** in verse 8. What a servant of God does affects not only his own life and standing in a community, but it affects the whole church of Christ. Every thoughtless word spoken by a counselor reflects on the whole body of Christians with whom he is associated. And, most importantly, it reflects on the name of the Lord Jesus Christ.

Of course, we do not have **slaves** today in western society. But what Paul says in verses 9 and 10 has much to do with the business relationships of workers to their employers. There was a time when Christians were becoming hardened about their attitudes toward employers like many from the world. But as I write, times have become more difficult; jobs are scarce and even PhDs are out painting to earn a living. Yet, even under such circumstances, there are those who mouth off to their employers. Paul says, train them not to **talk back.** Moreover they should **submit** and **seek to satisfy them.** The tendency to rebel, to talk back and do as one pleases is great among workers. In our society, it is possible to go get another job if one is dissatisfied with his present employment. So, clearly,

Titus 2

10 They must not become involved in petty thefts, but demonstrate that they can be trusted in everything, so that in every way they may make the teaching of God our Savior inviting.

---

there is no excuse for such behavior. A slave had no such option, yet he was supposed to follow these directions too. There is no place for griping and complaining—a thing too often engaged in even by Christians. Counselees, having difficulties with their jobs, should always be quizzed about these matters which are so fundamental to becoming a good employee. In conjunction with the passages in Colossians and in Ephesians, the counselor will find detailed instructions to give to the counselee who is in trouble because of his tongue, his failure to submit or his unwillingness to seek to satisfy his employer.

In addition, there is the problem of **theft**. Our whole society would find that costs are much less if and when petty theft ceased. Much of the cost of manufacturing, servicing, etc., must go to the replacement of those things that are pilfered by employees. Christian counselors shouldn't think it beneath them to inquire about the possibility of theft, when discussing the conduct of employees at work. It is the task of the counselor to point out that the counselee must demonstrate to his employer that he can be **trusted in everything**. Counselees who invite scrutiny by employers, who are not sure of their trustworthiness, bring a bad name upon the Lord. And, they will find restrictions and other obstacles placed in their way at every point., making their tasks unenjoyable. Those who demonstrate an exemplary lifestyle, on the other hand, **make the teaching of God our Savior inviting.** Their lives provide a convincing argument for their words about Christ. When people see in them all the things they would wish to see, they will more readily listen to their witness for Christ.

Now, of course, there are qualifications to the injunction to **submit... in everything**. Clearly, that injunction does not include acts of sin. If and when an employer asks an employee to sin (something God never granted him the authority to do), he must graciously refuse. If an employee has made himself invaluable to his employer, by doing those things that have already been mentioned, it will be only in rare instances that an employer will fire him for refusal. Counselors must make it clear that this refusal should carry none of the overtones of "I am holier than thou." Rather, it might be of the greatest benefit for the employee to suggest to his boss that there is another way to achieve the same purpose apart from lying, cheating, or whatever the sinful instruction involved. When the

Christian Counselor's Commentary

> 11 God's saving grace has appeared to all sorts of people,
> 12 training us to turn down irreligion and worldly desires and to live seriously and righteously and in a godly way in the present age,

---

employee's creativity in the matter is insufficient to come up with an alternative, the counselor who brainstorms with him about the matter can be of great assistance.

Turning now to a summary statement for all the classes that have been singled out, Paul talks about the resources that God has provided for attaining the ends that He prescribed. These resources can be capsulized in the fact that the same saving grace that God extended to bring about the conversion of the saints to whom Titus was to minister is available as sanctifying grace as well. That **saving grace** was found in Christ who **appeared to all sorts of people.** It was not restricted to one nation or class. What is saving grace? Grace means unmerited favor, as most Christians know. But there is a second meaning to the word: it also means help from God that is undeserved. It is help to achieve what God wants accomplished that one, by his own wisdom and power, is unable to achieve. And, the main means that God uses in assisting His children is to **train** them. This training is accomplished by the Holy Spirit using the Scriptures to instruct, correct, encourage and transform them.

Of what does such instruction consist? To **turn down irreligion and worldly desires**. That is the negative side of the training as it is here summed up. The positive side is **to live seriously and righteously and in a godly way in the present age** (v. 12). Two irreducible summaries of the work that Christian counselors, using the Scriptures, are involved in.

Counselors will find themselves constantly dealing with the problem of **worldly desires**. It is crucial to understand that worldliness is not a matter only of things one does or doesn't do. It is, primarily, an attitude. It is, as Paul put it, a matter of **desire**. James tells us that when we are tempted we are led astray by our own desires. These desires grow up in every sinful heart. But as they are gratified and encouraged they grow in intensity and frequency. As they are countered by Scripture that teaches the biblical alternatives, they grow weaker. Counselors will get nowhere with helping their counselees change their lifestyles until they learn to address the matter of their desires. Clearly, one of the things Christ came to do for those who trust Him as their Savior is to train them to **turn down** the **irreligion** that is the result of indulging in sinful desires. The body learns to want (desire) to do those things that the sinful nature has trained

13 expectantly awaiting the joyous hope, even the appearance of the glory of our great God and Savior Jesus Christ,

---

it to do. These response patterns become habitual. It is, therefore, essential to *retrain the body to desire those things that please God.* That is a matter of rehabituating the body (reprogramming the brain according to Scripture) and achieving new skills that are built into all other bodily structures as well (For more information on this, see comments on Romans, chapters 6, 7).

Living seriously, righteously and in a godly way has been discussed sufficiently already. It is important, nevertheless, to note Paul's careful emphasis on **this present age.** That is the age in which he and Timothy were ministering. And, it was an age in which (like every other age prior to the coming of Christ) the world (society as organized against God) dominates. What form that age takes in any given era is different. Basically, all is the same, but the forms of expressing and engaging in irreligion differ. Distinct problems address each era. That means that, to be a good counselor, one must study the era in which he lives so as to understand and detect the subtleties of sin and error as they are incorporated into the lifestyles of those whom he counsels. To be an effective counselor, then, is to know how to train the counselee in that lifestyle set forth in the Bible *as it pertains to the problems of the era in which he lives.*

There is another aspect to the positive side of the counselor's task: he must train his counselees to **expectantly await the joyous hope, even the appearance of the glory of our great God and Savior Jesus Christ** (cf. I Thessalonians Chapter One). One who learns to live in the light of that expectation, lives differently. He no longer sets his hopes on things that are transient; he looks for a city that has foundations. He no longer looks for the approval of men; he cares only to hear the voice of his Lord saying "Well done, you good, faithful servant." Everything is different. There is joy in the future—no matter how gloomy things my seem in the present age. The time is coming when **Jesus** will be acknowledged for whom He really is—**the great God and Savior**. And, your counselee, along with him, will receive acknowledgment as a child of God. There is **glory** coming **at His appearing** that will overshadow all hurts and problems and even death itself. Counselees who are counseled in this context, and who accept it as a fact for which they long, respond differently from those who do not. Counselor, how often do you speak about the coming of Christ when counseling? Think about that. The next time counseling seems dull

14 Who gave Himself for us to redeem us from all iniquity and to cleanse for Himself a people who are all His own, zealous for fine deeds.

or tragic, brighten the room with a discussion of Christ's appearing in glory.

Interestingly, when Paul sets forth the objective of the coming and death of Christ, he does not say "to redeem us." Instead, he says **to redeem us from all iniquity and to cleanse for Himself a people who are all His own, zealous for good deeds.** In that larger explanation, Paul expresses the divine intention in the salvation of His people. God wants a people who honor Him by their lifestyles. And He did not want people who grudgingly do His will. He sent Christ to die for the sins of people who, once having been cleansed by His blood, would become **zealous for good deeds.** That fact should greatly interest Christian counselors. When you talk to counselees, counselor, what do you so often find? Reluctance? Hesitancy? Unwillingness? Excuse-making? Grudging obedience? Well, what God wants is nothing less than **zeal** in obeying His will and engaging in holy living. To the extent to which you are willing to settle for anything less will determine the amount of effective Christian living your counsel will produce. You must be zealous yourself in the pursuit of holiness for your counselees, if you wish them to become zealous too. That means an enthusiasm for truth; it means settling for nothing less than what the Scriptures require. It means holding out high standards and objectives, never trimming your sails. It means expecting that the Holy Spirit, Who indwells every true believer, is capable of doing such things.

Then, concluding this chapter, Paul tells Titus to counsel and preach the things that he has so far explained. And with that teaching, he is to **urge, and convict** with **recognition that** [he has] **full authority to give orders**. Now, it is important to understand that an ordained minister of the Lord Jesus Christ counsels with authority. He is to be heard because of the One whom he represents and, of even greater significance, because he brings a message from God. Anyone who fails to counsel from the Scriptures is bereft of true authority. Those who use the Word can call counselees to obedience. No one can call them to obey Freud, Skinner, Maslow or Ellis! Legitimate authority comes from God alone. What warrant does anyone have for counseling another human being?

Full authority to help people change! Think of it. Counselors of every other stripe lack that authority. There is a factor never to be forgotten. While we **urge**—never wanting to simply assert bare authority—we

> 15 Speak these things; urge and convict, with recognition that you have full authority to give orders. Let nobody disregard you.

also convict when counselees fail to listen to the truth of God. The two must be used, usually in the order given. Indeed, Paul gave Titus full authority **to give orders**. Now, of course, this did not allow him to order people around according to his own whims. The orders were about those "things" (matters) of which he was to speak. In other words, counselors may not make up legalistic additions that they order counselees to follow, but they may surely say to them "You must **stop committing adultery.**" They may give that order on the basis that it is a clear command of Scripture. Even when they suggest ways and means not explicitly spelled out, but that are in harmony with and grow out of the Scriptures, they must never place these on the same level as the Scriptures themselves. Authority to order is the authority to order men to obey God's Word.

Finally, Titus (you) may never allow people to disregard him (you). When Paul told Timothy to let no one despise his youth, he used the word *kataphroneo ("to think down, despise")*. Here, he uses the word *periphroneo ("to think around")*. Counselors must be ready for both experiences—people trying to dodge the teaching of Scripture by directing criticism to the person ("You're too young to understand") and by avoiding you. This is done in counseling in many ways: by "misunderstanding" what you say, by taking the edge off of a sharp truth, by throwing off what you say as irrelevant, impossible etc. Counselors must learn to handle such dodges. God commands it!

CHAPTER 3

> **1** Remind them to submit to rulers and authorities, to obey them and to be ready to participate in every good activity,

In Chapter Three, Paul turns from specific groups to the entire membership to which Titus was to minister. He begins with a reminder: **remind them to submit to rulers and authorities**. Good teachers go over things again and again until they are sure that their students have a repeatable grasp of what they are saying. Counselors, dealing often with people confused and unable to assimilate what they need to know very well, would be smart if they followed this practice. It is easy to forget, to get things wrong in the first place or to hear only a part of what was said. Paul, in his wisdom, therefore, reminds Titus to remind his hearers to submit to the **authorities**.

It is an important area of life to which Paul addresses his remarks (He makes a point of the matter also in Romans 13 as does Peter in I Peter 2:13ff). The two terms used include all those who have any sort of official governmental positions. As the actions of tens of thousands of Christians who died rather than worship the genius of the Roman emperor testify, it is apparent that the admonition is not absolute. While all legitimate authority is from God, the authority He gave did not include the right to command a subject to sin.

That exception is clear, and applies to each of the four authority spheres mentioned in the Bible. These authority/submission spheres set forth are the Church, Marriage, Work and the State. God requires submission to those who have authority in these spheres so long as they exercise authority in accordance with the limited scope of authority given to the sphere itself. The authority given to those who rule in one sphere is not coextensive with the authority to those who rule within another. These do not overlap. This fact is absolutely essential for counselors to understand when dealing with matters that have dimensions in more than one sphere. Obedience to the state includes obeying irksome laws and taxes.

In counseling, one occasionally runs up against problems that a counselee is having with the government. He should be zealous in **reminding** the counselee of his obligation to **submit** to the government in the payment of taxes, etc. If he does not know the laws involved in some relationship of his counselee to the authorities, he should be careful to

Titus 3

2 to insult nobody, not to be quarrelsome; to be gentle, demonstrating full consideration for every person.

---

urge him to obtain legal counsel to be sure he is squeaky clean in the matter. Christians, like their Lord, and like the apostles, must **obey** the government—even when it makes foolish requirements—so long as the government does not ask them to sin.

And, whenever the government (or anyone else, for that matter) sponsors something that is a **good activity**, he should not stand aloof, but should lend his support to it. This command would refer to blood drives, disaster relief, etc. Christians, too often, do fail to **participate** when they should. Because of God's restraining grace, sinners do not fully realize their potential for evil. Even unbelievers, on a humanistically-driven basis often reach out to those in need. So, when the government or others (though here he is thinking of governmental activities) engage in socially good activities, Christians must be prepared to become involved. Christians should vote and hold public office should the opportunity arise. Joseph and Daniel are examples of how God can place a believer in high places—for His ends.

There are times when Christians may not participate in government-sponsored activities such as giving out condoms at schools or allowing their children to become part of school promoted new age programs). The believer participates only in those things that are *good*. And that means good according to God's standard, the Bible. Because it is not always easy to distinguish between the good and the bad counselors will frequently be called upon to help counselees make decisions.

Christians should **insult no one**. Not even those who are wrong or foolish. When you discover what is going on all around you, and when you are continually disappointed in others, it is easy to become cynical and, as a result, insulting when you talk to them. God will not allow that among those who are to be **zealous**—not in hurling insults but—**to do good deeds**.

Quarrelsomeness is taboo for believers. There is much that is wrong, much that must be exposed and withstood, but in all of it one must maintain the right spirit. Counselees who insult others ordinarily are also quarrelsome. The two sins ride in tandem. In sessions, therefore, counselors must not allow insults to be propelled toward others. Subdue the quarrelsome approach. Rather than invite such things (as some counselors do) encourage a truly Christian atmosphere in which to counsel. Prohibition

Christian Counselor's Commentary

3 At one time we too were foolish, disobedient, deceived, and enslaved to various desires and pleasures, going along through life with malice and envy, hated by others and hating them.

---

of these things does not curtail the telling of hard truth, but only sinful ways of doing so.

What sort of attitude pervades your counseling room? After reminding a counselee over and over again about his tongue, finally, I must say, "If you won't learn to mind your speech, I shall have to terminate counseling. One of the reasons you are here is precisely because of the attitudes you now are displaying. If there is one hour during the week when you will talk to one another as Christians should, it is during this hour. Now...if you are ready, let's continue. Tell her in a plain, non-insulting manner what it was you were about to say."

There are better ways for Christians to deal with wrongdoing—namely, by helping the one doing wrong to repent and do right. Nor are they to be **quarrelsome**. Often Christians bring opprobrium on themselves by the way they argue with unbelievers. While this does not refer to abandoning a proper defense of the faith, it does mean that he doesn't try to push his faith down others' throats. And, he doesn't pick verbal fights. Rather, on the positive side, he is **gentle**. That refers to his way with others. He is neither rough nor crude in his dealings with the world. He remains a gentleman in all that he does. And, he gives every person's viewpoint **full consideration.** He doesn't speak before he has heard the pertinent facts. Without participating in it himself, he is able to be stimulated to thought even by wild and useless speculation. He can find something in every person to which to react positively, even if it is to reject what he has to say in favor of the opposite (about which he might not have thought if the other person had not stated his view). Of course, no better advice could be given to a counselor himself than that found in verses 1 and 2. If the counselor fails to give full consideration to his counselee's ideas, however bizarre they may be, he will rarely be able to help him. He remembers Proverbs 18: 13, 15, 17.

One additional reason for this sympathetic attitude toward others is because you remember that, at one time, you too wore the same size shoes. But someone took the time and consideration to lead you to Christ. That is the thought that brings Paul to verse 4.

What you hear everywhere these days—unfortunately, even from many Christians, who counsel, is that what happened in your past is deter-

Titus 3

4 But when the goodness and deep affection that God our Savior has for people appeared, He saved us,

minative not only of what you are, but also of what you will be; that the past so determines the future that there is little in the present that can be done about it. If our Christian faith teaches anything, it is that this notion is utterly false. Though "sin abounds," according to Romans 5:20, "grace far more abounds." It is of the essence of Christianity to believe that there is no such determinism by circumstances, training, etc. When this domination of the past occurs it is not because it must but because one allows it to do so. God can, and does, move into the lives of men and women to transform them. If you don't believe that—why counsel? For that matter, why become Christians? Christians *must* maintain that sanctification (growth from sin to righteousness) is not only taught in the Bible, but is achievable in life. Verses 3 and 4, in a powerful way, proclaim this truth.

Looking backwards, Paul writes, **At one time we too were foolish, disobedient, deceived, and enslaved to various desires and pleasures, going along through life with malice and envy, hated by others and hating them.** What a graphic description of the unsaved lifestyle! The pagan life described here closely corresponds to that found in Ephesians 4:17-19 (esp., 19). It is a life of slavery to sin. So far, the idea of the past controlling the future is correct. And yet, there is no question that Paul believed that this slavery was over (cf. Romans 6, 7). He writes of being "dead" to sin, of being "freed" from its "dominion" and "power," and made alive to "newness of life." I have discussed this matter in some depth in my book, *The War Within* (Harvest House, Eugene: 1990), but see also, Romans, chapters 6-8 of this present commentary series. But don't miss the fact that he now distantiates himself from those who still live that way: **at one time we too were...**Paul has changed. He is no longer the man he used to be; he is not enslaved to the past. The chains are broken—he is free.

What Paul is saying is vital to Christian counseling—that the power of the Word and the Spirit are greater than all our sin. He maintains that various sinful desires and pleasures to which we were **enslaved** need no longer control if we are willing to put off the old ways and put on their biblical alternatives (cf. Ephesians 4). Christ has overcome the evil one and broken the reign of sin in the believer's life. While he may not yet have availed himself of them, all the resources necessary to live a life pleasing to God are his for the taking. On this, cf. I Peter 1:18ff., and com-

5 not because of deeds that we did in righteousness, but according to His mercy through the washing of regeneration and renewal, that come from the Holy Spirit,
6 Whom He poured out effusively on us through Jesus Christ our Savior

---

ments on those verses.

If a counselee maintains that he cannot change because of what has happened to him in the past, because the lifestyle out of which he came was too sinful and because of what others have done to him, this is one of the many verses to which you may turn to show him otherwise. It is not necessary to continue **to go along through life** as one did in the past.

How do we know that this is true? Verse 4 contrasts the impact of the first coming of Christ with the influence of the Christian's past. Because of God's **goodness** and **deep affection** we have been **saved**—not only from eternal damnation, but preeminently (in this place he emphasizes) from the foolish and harmful practices and desires of the former life. Here is your warrant for counseling: out of His tender love God dramatically changes people by releasing them from the grip of the past to enter into newness of life. It is the ministry of the Word, in the power of the Spirit, by which this takes place. And that ministry involves the personal application of the Word to individual problems; a process that we call *Christian counseling*.

Paul is so grateful for God's grace that he must remind Titus (and those looking over his shoulder as he reads) that the wonderful possibilities of a new lifestyle are not because of anything within us, but purely the result of God's good **grace** (vv. 5, 6). It is the **pouring out** of the Holy Spirit into the life of the Christian at regeneration (cf. Rom. 5:5) that makes this new life possible. There is no potential within the believer (apart from the Spirit) that can bring it off. But the **Spirit**—God Himself indwelling His people and His church—is greater than all our sin. That is why it is possible to make dramatic life changes. That is why a vacillating, impetuous, cowardly Simon can become a valiant, firm Peter. That is why a proud, demanding Pharisee named Saul can become a humble, serving Paul. That is why your counselee, steeped in the sinful patterns of the past can become a vital Christian living faithfully for his Lord. This you must believe, brother, sister, if you are to become an effective Christian counselor. And, this is the hope that you must instill in the heart and mind of your counselee as you begin counseling. **REGENERATION LEADS TO RENEWAL**. Perhaps you should frame that saying for your wall.

7 so that by being justified by His grace we might become heirs to the hope of eternal life.
8 This is a trustworthy saying

And, as verse 6 underlines, the gift of the Holy Spirit was no paltry thing, but, rather, he was **poured out effusively.** In other words, there is no reason for anyone to say that he needs something more. No, he already has all he needs through Jesus Christ. He does not need something more; what he needs is to use more of the something he already has. His problem is not the lack of resources, but a failure to fully appropriate and apply all that he has. There is no way, then, for your counselee to squirm out of his responsibility to change in ways that please God. God has done all that is necessary to effect that change; he can blame no one else if he refuses to acknowledge this or fails to access those more-than-adequate resources.

Now, it is not the counselor's task to change his counselee; that is the work of the Spirit, through His Word. The counselor may teach his counselee about what God has provided in Christ, show him how to access these resources and help and encourage him to do so. But the counselor is merely God's agent, ministering the Scriptures, used by the Spirit of God. He must point him to the true source of power.

And change begins when a believer is **justified by His grace** and becomes an heir to the **hope of eternal life.** Again, living in the light of the hope (remember, biblical hope is expectancy of a certainty) of an eternity with Christ, where all wrongs will be righted, where all suffering will be ended, and where all doubts, fears and tears will be banished, makes a great difference in how one chooses to respond to problems in the present. That focus on the future is altogether important. One who anticipates inheriting a fortune in the future lives differently today than the one who has no such hope (anticipation). The believer is an **heir to eternal life**! Reemphasizing this in counseling—especially when the counselee is pressing his nose hard against the present—can make all the difference in how one responds to difficulties, losses, trials, etc. Paul wants everyone to know that there is no uncertainty about what he has just affirmed, so he explains, **This is a trustworthy saying**. Thank God that something, somewhere, in this shaky, uncertain world of counseling is dependable! And Christian counselor—it is yours.

Paul continues: **insist on these things.** His use of the strong verb is instructive. There are things about which the counselor may not be hesi-

Christian Counselor's Commentary

> 8b Now, I want you to insist on these things with assurance so that those who have believed in God may make it their business to engage in fine deeds. These things are good and useful to people.

tant or equivocal; he must "insist" on them. This note adequately accompanies previous comments about authority, not allowing others to "think around" his teaching and giving orders. There **is** authority in the eldership and it is to be exerted whenever necessary. Christ has invested His own authority in the leadership of the church (cf. John 20:21-23). Counselors must never flaunt this authority, but neither may counselees ignore or dismiss it. Extremes on both sides must be avoided. But just because problems exist is no reason to reject a valid use of authority. Indeed, no effective counseling can be done without it. When persuasion, encouragement, instruction and all other less authoritative means fail, the counselor must exercise Christ's authority. That so much is made of the point in this letter indicates that Paul knew the Cretans and expected Titus to find a number of them digging in their heels. The phenomenon is not unknown today; the problem (possibly with Titus as well) is a reluctance to exercise biblical authority to its full when needed.[1] Titus (and every Christian counselor after him) is to insist that the members of the churches must obey the apostolic injunctions in this letter, but not just that; he was to insist on this **with assurance**. There is to be no half-hearted-because-uncertain-about-its-validity use of authority. Titus was to speak authoritatively according to what Paul had written. So, too, may any good biblical expositor-counselor today because his authority is not his own, but that of the Lord Jesus revealed in the Bible.

The purpose for this authority is to bring about good works among those who believe (v. 8^b). This is the same purpose that the biblical counselor pursues in all that he does. He wants the lifestyle of his counselee to conform to biblical standards *in order that his life may glorify his Father in the heavens*. Whenever a counselor forgets this purpose (the very theme of the Book of Titus) his counsel will be given in a way that harms rather than helps the counselee, if the latter accepts it. The task of counseling

---

1. Although, this emphasis on the use of authority may be designed to alert the Cretans to the fact that Paul had commissioned Titus to use apostolic authority to the full. In other words, Paul may have been here writing as much to the Cretans looking over Titus' shoulders as to Titus himself.

9 But avoid stupid arguments, questions about genealogies, strife and battles over the law, because these are useless and worthless.

must always exhibit pastoral concern. What Titus must insist upon, whether they acknowledge it or not, is not only **good** (that is, right) but also **useful.** The moment a counselor begins to study or employ the Scriptures in an academic rather than pastoral fashion he will begin to misuse them. The Bible was not intended to be debated academically in theological tomes; it was intended to be used to transform lives. Solid discussion of the meaning of passages, therefore, must always have as its underlying purpose (and approach) the benefit of the people of God to His glory.

Well, Titus has been told what to insist upon; now Paul tells him what to **avoid.** Stupid arguments are those that have no edifying results. Neither Jesus nor the apostles hesitated to argue their points—when the outcome was crucial to understanding of the Word of God and its application to life. But they engaged in no speculative debates. Nor should you. To do so, Paul says, is **stupid**. He now enumerates some of the sorts of things that would be stupid to become involved in. First, **questions about genealogies.** Again, we become aware of the large percentage of Jewish converts in the groups to which Titus was to minister. This sort of discussion—about who belonged to which tribe, and what the consequences might be for knowing so—was a peculiarly Jewish problem. There are, of course, very different problems today with which counselees could divert the discussion from vital matters to inconsequential ones. But, the principle remains the same. There are times when counselors—as Paul does here—must put certain discussions off limits.

But, the problem can become more difficult, because **strife and battles over the law also may** arise. True interpretation of the Scriptures is important since it is God's Word that sanctifies (John 17:17). Here one must distinguish between those arguments that are fought over Scripture that are pastorally relevant and those that are not—that are mere academic exercises. The latter, he says, are **useless and worthless,** and must be avoided. Counselees often try to drag the counselor into such battles. Foolish counselors take the bait and soon become bogged down in worthless discussion that does no one any good. Wise counselors will argue only for those things vital to the counseling process. Wisdom and discernment are needed to make good decisions here. Why no go over your notes from the last ten counseling cases that you conducted and try to determine what items you discussed that should have been eliminated? It would be

Christian Counselor's Commentary

10 After counseling him once or twice, give up on a divisive person, and have nothing more to do with him,
11 knowing that this sort of person is twisted and is self-condemned by his sinful ways.

---

interesting, also, to determine how much time was lost on foolish wrangling, and in how many cases people failed to receive help because of unnecessary fighting between you and them over nonessentials.

Paul now anticipates a problem he often encountered in his counseling practice among members of the churches—the schismatic. Even before the churches on Crete had been organized, therefore, Paul outlines specific measures to take if and when possible incitements to schism may arise. A **divisive person** must be dealt with summarily. If he isn't dealt with quickly he will split your church before you know it! He is to be **confronted in counseling once or twice**. There is to be no long, drawn out process of dealing with him. If his presence is very divisive, one session is enough before putting him out of the church (**have nothing more to do with him**). If there seems to be some hope of turning him around take a second shot at it. But, under no circumstances, are you to go on and on, all the while giving him a platform for his nefarious activities. He should not receive even the normal amount of time allotted for counseling. Remove him from a place of influence as soon as possible. Many churches have been destroyed by failure to observe this command to the letter. Thinking they knew better than God, they spend long periods of time working with people, whose only purpose in prolonging counseling was to give them more opportunity to influence others in the congregation. Actually, in order to save the one, they hurt the many. Alert counselors readily become aware of divisive attitudes among counselees. Upon detecting these, they must warn them of the impending danger of being "handed over to Satan" in church discipline. The exhortation at this point is a practical application of the passage in Proverbs 22:10.

It is not even necessary to hold a trial; this sort of person **condemns himself** (v. 11). His purposes are so twisted and his sinful ways are so obvious, that in the eyes of the elders of the church he clearly reveals his basic divisiveness. If there is any slight uncertainty, that is one reason for holding one or two counseling sessions with him.

Incidentally, it is interesting to note that one or two sessions is considered a *brief* number of sessions—counseling is shortened to eliminate divisive persons before they do more harm. That must mean that the apos-

12 When I send Artemas or Tychicus to you, do your best to come to me in Nicopolis, since I have decided to spend the winter there.
13 Do your best to supply everything that Zenas the lawyer and Apollos need for their trip; be sure they lack nothing.

---

tle envisioned ministers of the Word usually (in the counseling of nondivisive persons) spending more than this minimum number of sessions with a counselee. Some who have not found a number of sessions listed in the Bible foolishly conclude that all sessions are single ones. This verse shows that to be a false conclusion.

Over the years, we have found more than 12 weekly sessions ordinarily to be unproductive, but, in about six, if the counselee is cooperative and the counselor is doing all the right things, the problem should be turned around (that does not always mean fully solved, but well on the way toward a solution). Most cases last around 8 or 9 weeks, maximum. Some counselors treat everyone as if their problems could be solved in one or two sessions. This passage shows that Paul thought otherwise and should disabuse you of any such idea.

Now, Paul comes to his concluding remarks.

Paul is always concerned about the work everywhere. And in supervising a team of men who ministered throughout the Mediterranean world, of which he was the leader, he seems always organized. Here he is arranging matters, even as he does in other letters. He is going to send two others to take Titus' place (v. 12). Presumably, Paul wanted Titus to organize the churches and then move on to other things, while Artemas and Tychicus would continue to work with them regarding problems that might arise and in doing all they could to strengthen the churches. He is interested in conferring with Titus, doubtless, about how the ministry in Crete panned out and other matters that are unspecified. He also talks about Titus supplying **Zenas the lawyer** (not all Christian converts were nobodies) and **Apollos** for their coming **trip**—they must **lack nothing**. How all this was to work, we can only speculate. Where were Zenas and Apollos? Were they with Titus? Were they stopping by Crete on their way somewhere else? We just don't know.

What, then, are we to make of verses 12 and 13? Simply this: it is important for the people of God to do all they can to forward the work of Christ, particularly as this pertains to the work of spreading the gospel. Selfish counselees need to gain a larger perspective than their own concerns. So often those who come for counseling are wrapped up in them-

Christian Counselor's Commentary

14 Let our people learn to engage in fine deeds to meet pressing needs so that they may not be unfruitful.

15 All who are with me greet you; greet our affectionate friends in the faith.
May help be with all of you.

---

selves: they have few interests other than their problems, and their so-called "needs." It is important in counseling to enlarge their interests, and turning them to such missionary interests at home or abroad as can occupy their time, prayer and funds may be precisely what would do it. At all costs, be on the alert for this difficulty in counselees; problems tempt one to focus inwardly. Frequently, along with other difficulties that you will face, this will surface as a complicating problem.

In summary, once again returning to his theme, Paul urges **our people** (a warm term of affection) **to engage in good deeds to meet pressing needs so that they may not be unfruitful** This emphasis is entirely in harmony with what I have been observing in verses 12, 13. How easy it is for a counselee to become utterly fruitless through pursuing his own interests. Counseling can contribute to this phenomenon. All the while that one is dealing with the counselee's situation, it is mandatory for him to keep the focus on what the counselee is doing for others (**good deeds**). And, surely, in our day, no less than in Paul's, there are many **pressing needs**. It is in meeting those needs—some of which, we have seen are in the area of missions—that this balancing factor is best found. It might not be a bad policy for you to give each counselee who seems self-oriented the assignment of listing a dozen pressing needs that *others* have. From these you could help him choose one or two that he could **meet.** It is not wrong to help a counselee begin to become fruitful along with whatever other matters you and he must address. As a balance to the self-focus required by counseling, this is a worthy emphasis.

Then, a last farewell: **Greetings** from those here to those there, says Paul. He was always concerned to keep fostering the fellowship of Christians located in various places. The warmth of the man emerges in the words **greet our affectionate friends in the faith**. In all counseling, it is your task to promote fellowship among believers. Think of ten ways that you can use a portion of the counseling hour to do just that. His parting words are a wish for **help** to all in Crete—a wish appropriate to every church and all Christians everywhere.

CONCLUSION

Obviously, Titus is not a book principally concerned with counseling, but it does contain much that counselors and counselees must learn. It is my hope that in perusing this volume, and as you turn to Titus from time to time, you will have a deeper appreciation for the pastoral concerns of the great apostle Paul that have reference, either directly or indirectly, to the task of the Christian counselor. There is much there both in terms of direction and inference about what to and how to do it. I trust that as you do return to Paul's letter, with a counseling eye cocked toward it, you will continue to glean insights into counseling that will benefit you and those you counsel.

www.ingramcontent.com/pod-product-compliance
Lightning Source LLC
LaVergne TN
LVHW051245080426
835513LV00016B/1753